The Birth of Hip Hop

THE BIRTH OF HIP HOP

"Rapper's Delight"—
The Gene Anderson Story

by GENE ANDERSON

Transcribed and Edited by
Christina E. Stock

Published by Amorphous Publishing Guild
Buffalo, NY USA
www.Amporphous.Press

AmorphousPublishingGuild

This book is dedicated to everyone in St. Louis, and throughout the world, who hustled – recording, performing, distributing, DJing, and promoting the genre's earliest records – to push Hip Hop into the mainstream of music and entertainment.

Without you, Hip Hop as we know it would not exist.

Contents

Acknowledgements

I would like to acknowledge these magnificent people and wholeheartedly thank them for their contributions to my book and my story, *The Birth of Hip Hop: "Rapper's Delight"–The Gene Anderson Story*. But first, I would like to thank God for giving me the opportunity to write this book, to live this story, and be able to pass it on for those who have a love for the art form of Hip Hop.

Thanks to the Robinson family – Joe Robinson, Sr., the Queen, Sylvia Robinson, Joey Robinson, Jr., and the entire Robinson family – for loving me so much and allowing me the opportunity to be the first one to deliver their hit record, "Rapper's Delight."

I would like to thank Skip Gorman and his family, and Harold Goldman and his family, for believing in me and starting the record distributing company, Midwest Record Distributors, in St. Louis. They gave me an opportunity to do it my way and we, together, kicked off the biggest music genre of all time–Hip Hop.

I would like to thank the Hudson family, Ted and Zelda Hudson, for being there for me when I was so confused about what to do next to promote these records, against all the obstacles that was in our way–because nobody really wanted to deal with rap records, as they were known then. They was always there to make me kick it up another notch, to move on, and do what I had to do. And together, we made a lot of big rap stars.

I would like to thank Dr. Jockenstein (Rod King), Jim Gates, Curtis Soul, Randy OJ, Big Ralph Little, and all the other DJs and friends from WESL radio in East St. Louis. They made it happen first for me.

I would like to thank Melvin Jones, Pervis Spann, E. Rodney Jones, Dale Rice—DJs around the Midwest that played these records for me under duress. People said they was not gonna work, and "don't play 'em no more." They played 'em anyway.

I would like to thank my friend, Gerry Ralston. He was the first guy that pushed me hard to write this book. I was a little apprehensive, but he knew that I had it in me and gave me all the support that I could receive from a friend. He passed me on to very capable people that made it all come together.

I would like to give a super special thanks to Christina Stock, the one that transcribed this entire book, and put it together with spit and bubble gum, to make sure it would be perfect and with love. She did a magnificent job. I will be forever thankful and love her for all of her efforts.

Another special thanks for Miss Loretta Turner. She did, as you can see, a magnificent job with her graphics on the jacket of this marvelous book.

Last but not least – as they say you save the best for last – Miss Sophia Stewart, known as the "Mother of The Matrix". Thank you so much for giving me advice on the release, the publishing, and the promotions of my book.

These people have contributed so much in my life, and for this book. Words can't express how I'm so appreciative of their sincerity and their love for me.

And I thank you, the reader, for taking the time to enjoy and get the real story, my story, on *The Birth of Hip Hop*.

Introduction

For years, people have asked me, "Why have so much concern and awareness for the art form of Hip Hop music?" not knowin' that it's part of my DNA. After you read this book, you'll find that there's more to the silk that's been held up by 2x4s to make this music that you call Hip Hop function.

It wasn't always as dazzling as it is today. Kids grow up today sayin' they're gonna be a Hip Hop artist, make millions, wear gold, and have millions of fans around the world—all the wonderful things that being a hip hop star now has to offer.

But, as I said, that's the "silk" of the Hip Hop genre. Now, the 2x4s that the silk is nailed on to—that's the history of how this business came about.

There was once a song that came out, called "Rapper's Delight," that changed the face of the stars and the type of entertainment that is now known as Hip Hop. That song made the world accept Hip Hop as being mainstream and legitimate. But there were times when this music was looked at as a fad. It would never make it. The last record would be the only one that they would play, and there would be no more on the radio.

Guys like me, and strong people that depended on records for survival – for their families and for their existence – were associated with companies like Sugar Hill, Enjoy, Tommy Boy, etc.. They were reaching out and pursued artists back in the early days of Hip Hop. They were strong in their beliefs that this art form would eventually catch on and could become mainstream. So, they seeked out small distributors in major areas that would hound their product and work their product in those areas, in hopes that this could grow and be big and create superstars like today.

When I came into the business, there was no hip hop business. I worked for some old Jewish guys—we created a company, and we received the first Hip Hop records (which were then called Rap records). To keep the doors open, we worked our asses off—to get 'em played, and to make the artists famous, so we could have another day with a paycheck.

They came and got me, started a company just for me. We created a promotion firm, and the rest is history. This book will explain, step by step, how it all happened. And I'm sure you will understand why my personal feelings about Hip Hop run so deep.

So now, enjoy my book—The Birth of Hip Hop: "Rapper's Delight"—The Gene Anderson Story.

Setting the Stage

This is a story of all stories, and it started with a guy by the name of Wonder Mike.

He started off by saying "a-hip-hop, a hippity-hop," and so forth and so on, not knowing that that phrase was the description of an entire cultural era that now exists, that has worldwide influence, named "Hip Hop."

I'd like to take you back to the beginning, where it all started.

I left Memphis, Tennessee and had a son, eight-years-old, named Petey. I already had a career as a soul singer. I had a wife, a "little thang." She was in my group. We had a little piece of a hit record called "Mixed Emotions", and we had done very good for a minute.

Then, all of a sudden, all hell broke loose. I got a divorce from my wife, and my son and I were on our own. In a way, this story is about my son.

I had been down to Memphis, Tennessee, with Willie Mitchell at Hi Records trying to make a career of it. Nothing was working, so I came back home and moved in with my mother and the baby. I was trying to find something to do so that we could just hang on and exist.

So I remember, back in the day, I was trying to put on some shows and was doing some independent music–cutting some records, some 45s. And I had some associates who were distributors down on Washington Street, which they used to call "Record Row."

I had went to see some old, Jewish friends of mine who had started in the record distributing business in the Midwest. Some of the guys had created big national chains like Mr. David Lieberman, who ended up with Lieberman's distributing company, and Mr. Hofstetter who had big distributors who were known around the world.

With my son, in front of Hi Records

(l-to-r) Hi Records; Willie Mitchell; Mabon "Teenie" Hodges; Gene Anderson; James Mitchell

There were small guys by the name of Pat Blonda, who had a one-stop shop. That was a shop that the mom-and-pop shops would buy from in order to be able to get their stock to sell to the customers in the neighborhood. All of the "Black" shops were primarily his customers.

At Pat's One Stop, all of the old guys that were in the record business used to hang out there. They used to hang out there in the back and play Gin Rummy and hope that they could find a record label to distribute to their people that had the big distributions that they knew.

It was a guy by the name of Skip Gorman, an old Jewish guy that I'd known, back in the day when I was trying to make records before, when I'd hit a lick and became a nationally known artist down with Mitchell at High Records. He was glad to see me, and he introduced me to another old Jewish guy who ended up having more influence on me in my understanding of the record business, and business in itself, and had a lot of influence on me in time. His name was Harold Goldman.

Mr. Goldman was a very fair person, and him and his brother had once created something called a "rack jobber." It had became such a profitable business. He was the one that created putting records in grocery stores, supermarkets, ten-cent stores, and anywhere with a rack. It became such a big, solid business that they gave it a name called "rack jobbing."

He sold out for a few million dollars, after years of being in that business, to some majors and he wasn't allowed to get back into the rack jobbing business for ten or twenty years. He was already an old man – 75 years old – but the record business is in the blood. It's just like anything else—if you once were in it big time, somehow you had to be around it, affiliated with it, or associated with it.

So, they all were hanging around with Pat Blonda and some old Jewish guys that had started in the record business back in the 78 (rpm) days and before. You know, it was just a thing that was a cultural association at that time.

And they liked me, so they would always pull me in the back room with all of them, and I was their boy. They just loved me because I had an extroverted personality, and they all knew me when I was a youngster really trying to make it. They knew I was one of the guys that had been halfway successful and that they felt they had halfway raised.

I was trying to ask them to find out some kind of way that I could get a job down there to take care of this kid. I didn't have no place to do nothing at, so I was hanging out with them.

Mr. Goldman wanted to get back in the business. Him and Skip were partners, and he just loved me from the first thought. So one day he asked me, "Jadie Boy, what would you like to do?"

I said, "If I can't do nothing else, I'd like to distribute my own records and promote 'em and get 'em out there."

He said, "I'll tell you what. I'll talk it over with Skip."

One day we went to lunch, Skip Gorman and I were talking about it. Mr. Goldman had the money, Skip had the know-how, and I had the energy, the excitement, and the motivation to make it happen.

Mr. Goldman got an office right next door to Pat's One Stop and created a distributor company by the name of Middle West Record Distributors. Skip called around to some of his old cronies, and they finally found a couple of records to give Skip to distribute that nobody else wanted to play with.

Skip knew how to put it all together, and Mr. Goldman had the money and so he was the boss. And he loved me, so when he got a building next door to Pat's and had offices there, he gave me my own office—my first office.

Skip had the office in the store room. Skip knew an Italian guy named Tony who had the hookups with the clubs and stuff. Pat gave us records from K.C. and the Sunshine Band and Donna Summers. Disco music had just hit, so we started something called "Disco Pool."

We were splitting distributions with that, so we were shipping out records to the different stores across the country that Skip knew, and those that were from the old books that he had from the company that he had worked deals with. Lieberman's distributing company ended up as one of the biggest distributors in the world.

It was four of them that started it, and Skip was one of the four. It was Norman Hofstetter, David Lieberman, Pat Blonda. More people started some independent distributors that ended up as some of the biggest distributors in the world.

They started business at St. Louis down there, out at Locust Street and Washington Avenue in St. Louis downtown. So Skip had some friends that were in business across the country and he was telling them that he had a little record here, and could he send them 100 copies and they would distribute a couple records here and there. But he was doing that and giving the records to me and Tony.

Tony had the big clubs, the big White clubs, that he would take the records over and distribute them. I would take them to the Black clubs over near St. Louis and Clayton and stuff.

So we were rolling for a while, and I started to get these brothers that would help me, as a distributor of records. They would give us a chance to get into the clubs free because we had some records to give to the DJ. The DJs would be looking for us and they'd come down to the distributing office, and down to the distributor's store on Washington, and we would give them free samples and they'd have new records to play.

We got a label from here and a label from there, and then all of a sudden we got lucky and got some hit records from some other small labels. It was going on pretty good, and I had my crew.

The Grind

I would go out to St. Louis at night. I had my mother's car, and we would stay out all night so I could never get back to work at 8 o'clock in the morning like Tony. So between Tony, who was doing the big disco clubs, and Skip, they would always try to sprinkle a little salt on me with Mr. Goldman.

Mr. Goldman had all the money – he was the bottom line – but Mr. Goldman knew the truth that I had more effect than Tony did because they were only playing records, but my records was being sold out of the store. I was promoting on the streets with me and my crew.

So Mr. Goldman wasn't gonna let Skip and Tony pile up against me, and so they always had a little animosity, for a moment. Then all of a sudden we started getting some records from some major companies that was doing that Disco thing. And they knew that there was something special going on out of St. Louis because records that wasn't being broken anywhere else seemed to be breaking out of St. Louis from our little small distributor. They didn't realize that it was me and my crew, and Tony and his crew. We had created something, and didn't realize it, called "The Disco Pool."

So we started calling companies up and having them send us some promotional records–a box or two which had 100, 50, or 75 of each record and we was passing 'em out to the different discos and to the different promoters and disc jockeys. They started coming by the distributing house to pick up some records on what was new. And I had all of the jocks in the Black areas coming to get them from me because nobody had never really given records out in a massive amount, as I was doing when we first started promoting these records, trying to get our name into the streets as the DJ-friendly distribution house, Middle West Record Distributors.

So all of a sudden, out of the different records we was getting from different companies, we started working with this guy by the name of Joe Robinson, who was a friend of Skip, that I had heard about through different people, disk jockeys and stuff. In the record business, he was sort of like the Al Capone of the record business of the Black side of town.

He owned a company by the name of All Platinum Records and had been in business a long time and he was having a discrepancy between him and a group called The Moments. The Moments was taking him to court and they couldn't put out no records under All Platinum. So they came up with another label by the name of Turbo. And they came out with different songs and stuff and I was trying to promote 'em but they finally came up with a group called Trouble Funk.

Trouble Funk was a go-go group from out of D.C. and they put their record out on Turbo. The record did pretty good but it really wasn't raising no hell for that label, and they were just barely hanging in there. And they used to be a major influence on the Soul/R&B record charts as a major label, as All Platinum. But this Turbo was a whole brand new adventure. So he put out a record on them and then he put out another record on them and it just didn't seem to work.

So one day, out of the clear blue sky, we gets a call from him and he talks to Skip. Him and Skip got to talking and Skip said, "Well, you need to talk to Gene about that."

I got on the phone and Joe introduced himself to me. I was overwhelmed 'cause I had heard some stories about Joe Robinson that was supernatural—like leaping off buildings in a single bound.

Joe Robinson was a big name in the black industry as far

as I was concerned, and he wanted to talk to me about a record they was cutting – the record wasn't even cut! – and he wanted to know what I thought about it.

I got on the phone with him and we chatted a while and laughed a while. I felt like Superman after I talked to Joe because here's Joe Robinson who wants to talk to me, Gene Anderson.

I didn't know that my reputation had leaked out across the country as the guy that was promoting the R&B records. I was taking records that nobody else could break and making some noise with 'em. They were looking for a hero, or a hero record, during that time and my name had leaked all the way up to Joe Robinson.

So we get to talking and he said, "Man, I've a got a new record, it's kinda like, something we call rappin'."

"Yeah?" I said, "Well send it on down."

He said, "Well I'm gonna send it down there to Skip, but I need to press at least 1,000 of 'em and Skip needs to come on and kick in some money to press the first thousand records of this record that I'm gonna send you."

"Well, Joe, I ain't got but a couple hundred dollars," I said, "But I'll talk to Skip and them and see what we can come up with and see if we can send you a thousand or two to press this record."

Because I knew that if Joe Robinson was asking us to help him promote and to manufacture these first records, this had to be a blister of a record–I mean a whopper of a record.

"Rapper's Delight"

At first, I'm thinking Joe sent over another record, just like Trouble Funk or the other stuff that he was doing normally. A few days later, I looked in the mail and a box came by UPS and it had about ten acetates (records made of acetate plastic) in it, and the label was written in red pencil writing. And the red pencil writing had on it "Rapper's Delight."

And I said, "Man, what is that?"

It was a 12-inch single and it didn't have no B-side, it was just one big, long record. It had time on it–15 minutes.

And I go, "15 minutes?! What the hell is that?"

So, we put the record on the record player and it started off, "Do-do-do..."

One of the biggest records of that time was disco called "Good Times" by Sheik. Before we could hear the record, we said, "That's Sheik! He cut Sheik."

Then all of a sudden we heard somebody say, "I said a hip hop, the hippie, the hippie, to the hip hip hop and you don't stop" on and on and on and on.

And I couldn't believe it, I said, "Man! What kinda shit is this?!"

Then it kept on, it said, "My man, Big Bank Hank"

And Big Bank Hank came up with, "If your girl starts actin' up, then you take her friend."

Boy, I cracked up and fell to the floor, and Skip and them were standing with Mr. Goldman with their mouths open talking about, "What's going on?"

First thing crossed my mind was that the boys in East St. Louis had sneaked up there to New York and cut a record from WESL because we was doing that kind of rap on the radio, live on WESL in the clubs.

And I thought it was a guy by the name of Jockenstein. Him, me, Curtis Soul, and all of them on Jim Gates's station, we was doing that shit live on the radio, but we was saying some other stuff. I thought that they had sneaked up there and cut a record without me that I was so mad I couldn't do.

So I called over to the station; nobody answered the station. And we started listening to the record.

Joe calls back and Joe said, "What do you think about the 'Rapper's Delight'?"

I said, "Man, is that Gates Jim and Jockenstein?"

He said, "No, them are some boys my son was going to school with, and Sylvia took 'em in the studio and cut 'em."

He said, "This is gonna be the biggest historical record in the world, Gene."

I said, "Joe, whatever it is, I'm with ya."

I talked to Skip and we sent Joe the thousand dollars.

Joe sent us the first 1,000 records along with a label was on 'em. It was a red label and on the label was "Rapper's Delight" and Sugar Hill Gang on it, Sugar Hill Records.

That's the first time we'd ever heard of that word and heard of that record.

Now, before we got those records in, I had those few acetates and I took 'em around. I was driving my mother's little car, and I rode over to WESL radio, where Gates was at. Gates had gotten a copy of the record from Dave Clark, an old veteran promotion guy, who gave the record to Gates because he didn't have time to promote the record. He never got a chance to promote the record at all, but he gave it to Gates.

"I've already got it. I got it right now..." Gates said, when I got there, "Matter of fact, I'm gonna play it all day. Everybody on my station's gonna have to play this record all day."

Now WESL was the kind of radio station that after 5

o'clock in the evening you could just barely hear it, but it was making so much noise and doing so many things in the neighborhood and stuff with that label. That station had so many jocks with personality, and we was doing live in the clubs.

We were outclassing the big stations with big watt power. Sometimes the station would have so much static that you could hardly hear it, but when it didn't, people loved it.

And we was rolling so hard with "Rapper's Delight" and every disc jockey played it that day and played it that night. It was playing so hard that people started calling in saying, "What's that? What's that?"

And the record was so long, so I took it to the clubs, I took it to the streets. I took it out to Gates and them, and I took it to all the mom-and-pop shops and let them hear the record. Everybody was going crazy about the record.

There wasn't no records for sale, we didn't have no records for sale, so they didn't have no place to put the record. As a matter of fact, they didn't have no rack to rack the records in because it was a 12-inch and we only had those little few disco records that were 12-inch. The record distributors and the record one-stops didn't have no place to put the record.

So Mr. Goldman went over there to Pat Blonda and told Pat, "I'll build you a rack so you can have some place to put these damn records, man, 'cause people are knocking the door down for these records. And some of the people we can't sell to direct because we're a distributor."

Pat put up a section, where Mr. Goldman took a hammer and put up a section where they were putting albums and named it, "Disco Racket."

And we put those records there, along with K.C. and them and Donna Summers's new records.

We didn't have the record up there for 2 hours and it was sold out.

Pat couldn't believe it, nobody could believe it. All of a sudden, because I had been out in the streets a night and a half, all the disc jockeys was coming in there sayin', "Man, we want a copy of the 'Rapper's Delight.'"

I didn't know what it was, but I was excited because I knew we had started something; we finally got a fire up in this little record distributor, Mid West.

Everybody, all the disc jockeys was coming in there, the street jocks, they all wanted a copy of this record. Then, all of a sudden, the record mom-and-pop shop owners was going past the One Stop, coming directly to us because Pat was selling them out as fast as he could get it.

Fueling the Fire

Now Mr. Goldman sends Joe $5,000. We was trying to get about 5-10,000 records right now 'cause Skip knows the business and he knows that this record here is on fire.

At this point, we was about to go out of business and needed to run our ass off with this record to keep the doors open. We was waitin' to see if Joe's gonna send us overnight the next shipment of records, because the record is burnin' hot right now.

So, I'm on the telephone calling around to some disk jockeys that I'd already met and known through some other things that I had done before I got with them. I called Dale Rice and KPRS.

I told Dale about the record, Dale said, "Man, I can't play no record 15-minutes long."

I said, "Dale, this is the biggest record in the world."

He said, "Well, just send it in. Let me see what you're talking about."

I sent the record to Dale overnight.

I called Melvin Jones down in Memphis, Tennessee. I'm never gonna forget it.

I said, "Melvin, I've got a new record, man. It's a rap record."

He said, "What's a rap record?"

I said, "They rap, like, 'Hip hop, the hippity hop...'"

I had it all messed up, backwards. I couldn't say what the phrases were.

"They're playin' those good times, the good times" I said, "That Sheik music, man. They're playing the good times, man. This is gonna be an elephant of a record."

He said, "Well, send it to me, Poo Poo."

I sent him the record, and a couple days later Melvin Jones was on the phone screamin'.

"Man! This is the biggest thing I ever heard in my life," he said, "People is goin' crazy."

Then "Boss Ugly Bob" called me at the record shop down there, in Memphis, Tennessee, called me and said, "Man, we need some of these records."

And I talked to Skip and Skip got hooked up with Boss Ugly Bob. All the distributors that I had known, that'd been trying to do my own little stuff through, they was callin' in—they wanted to talk to me.

All of a sudden, my name blew up like you wouldn't believe. I mean, in less than 72 hours this stuff was goin' on. The record was such a phenomenal success. I mean, now guys was comin' and knockin' on the distributor's door that we'd never seen before, wantin' to buy some "Rapper's Delight." We ain't got a copy.

Jim Gate's is jammin' down our throats. All we got is just the little promos that I had, around 10 or 15 or 20 copies left, and that's all that was in the house. We waitin' on the airport, because they shipped 'em in by airplane, 24 hours. We were waiting for the airplane, for the airport to call us in order to let us know that the records was there.

About that time, the radio stations, I was callin' KATZ, tryin' to get them to play the record. They were tryin' to play hard ball because WESL had the record first. We had already tried to get in touch with them, but they didn't wanna play the record because it was our little small distributor's record, and they ain't never been in love with me at that time. So, they was tryin' to play hardball. But Jim Gates was jammin' it down their throats.

Every jock on his station couldn't wait to get on the air and play that "Rapper's Delight," the long 15-minute version.

As a matter of fact, they could go to the toilet while the

record was bein' played and come back, go outside, smoke a joint of weed, come back in, and record was still playin'. Boy, they was having a ball with the record.

All of a sudden, kids were comin' over to the radio station and requesting the record and having a "Rapper's Delight" party in the parking lot while the record was playin' while the radio was playin' it. Now, everybody in town was callin' requesting the record.

This is the power of a legitimate, undisputed, hit record. I'd never experienced this before and, truthfully, I never experienced it after that, about that type of a record.

Next thing I knew, we finally got some records in. I had to go out there to the airport, me and Skip, and pick 'em up.

Tony's upset 'cause Tony ain't trying to promote no rap records. All he's interested in is disco records, because he was going to the big clubs and Mr. Goldman was giving him money to go out there and to hang with all the pretty girls at the disco clubs.

Tony was trying to hold back on this rap stuff, saying that this stuff was a fad. "It isn't gonna work long. Don't put nothing in it. Let's stay with this disco stuff because I'm getting cool with the DJs, and this pool is developing, and we can mail out a bunch of stuff to them, so..."

What he was really trying to do was to keep me out of the loop because he knew that I was getting money to go out at night and promote these records, and it was taking some money away from the money that he would be able to get.

But Mr. Goldman knew better, 'cause Mr. Goldman wasn't prejudice at all. Mr. Goldman, he was on my side because he really started that company because he liked me and wanted me to have something to do. So Mr. Goldman wouldn't pay no attention to Tony and gave me more money to work with.

One day, when the record was so big, guys was comin'

in the door and was buying boxes of 'em. Boxes of 50, and taking 'em out and putting 'em in the trunk of their car. And they were sellin' the records out of the trunk of their car, and coming back to buy another box 'cause the record didn't cost what I think was about $2.50, and they were selling 'em for $5. And that was cheaper than selling 'em for $15 or $20, which an album was selling for, and a 45 was selling for a dollar, but you could get $5 for just one record on a 12-inch, which was called a "disco plate."

Everybody was making money with the record. The guy down the street, I used to get a copy of them, I would tell 'em I need some promos and I'd get 50 copies of promos and say "I'm going out tonight to promote the record." I'd promote 10 records and sell all the rest of them and have a pocket full of money.

Everything was rollin', I'm doing fine. We didn't have the record 2-3 weeks and everybody in the country is calling us saying they heard about it and didn't know how to get the record—because they didn't know that Sugar Hill was the old All Platinum with Joe Robinson. So now my name is getting out there 'cause they're saying, "Who did you get the record from?"

"We got the record from Gene Anderson—Poo Poo Man."

"Where is he?"

"He's down at St. Louis with Midwest Record Distributors."

Now Melvin Jones got the record out to all of the clubs, 'cause I put him out and sent 5-10 records 'cause the record was so big. He started passing the record out to the club owners and stuff down in Memphis, Tennessee.

Now the record's hot and, son of a gun, Jim Gates is on fire. Just about everyone in town and across the country is talking about WEFL. Jim Gates is doing his thing; I'm doing my thing. Jockenstein and all of them was in the clubs: I've got Randy OJ; I got Big Time Frank; I got Curtis Soul; I got all of the DJs that's out there in the streets.

Everybody's playing the "Rapper's Delight." You go from one club to another club and there ain't nothing playing but the "Rapper's Delight."

Everywhere you go you hear, "Bum bum bum bum, a hip hop..."

Boy this shit is going on. Now my name is growing in town and growing outside of town.

Here comes a guy by the name of Deke Atkins from out of Chicago. He comes in town and tells everybody, "Hey! I'm the one that started that record." Everybody, we ran him out of town.

"Boy, you ain't started no record! We been had that record going on before you showed up!"

So, Deke was a little gangster from outta Chicago, and he was real tight with Joe and them because Joe... You know—"Birds of a feather fly together," and Deke was in their "fly together" crew, more or less. But Joe knew in his heart that I was the one who got this record started.

Now all of a sudden he calls us up says, "Hey, man. We got another group called Sequence. I've got a record that I think is gonna be huge—it's called, 'We gonna funk you, right on up, we gonna funk you right on up.'"

I took the record and didn't even have to have the record 5 hours. The record was playin' on every radio station. All of 'em but KATZ. They still hadn't gone on it yet because they were still trying to hold out—because they were trying to hold Gates and them down at WESL and to keep me not gettin' nowhere.

But the record took off. Next thing I knew I got another call from Joe. He got a record called, I think it was, Freedom, by Grandmaster Flash and the Furious Five. Or it was Happy Birthday. I can't remember which one was first. But he sent us a record by Grandmaster Flash and the Furious Five. Boy, that record took off.

Now, next thing I know, months had passed by. My name is burning up across the country.

"You guys gotta call Poo Poo Man, Gene Anderson, down at Midwest. He can break your records. He can break your records."

We get a call from a guy over at Mercury Records they say, "We got a record by a guy by the name of Kurtis Blow. It's called 'Christmas Rappin.'"

They sent me about ten copies I take it over here and there, took it over to the Regal Room over in East St. Louis. And, before you know it, Kurtis Blow was the first single artist to come up with a record of his own that was a rap record.

Boy, now I'm really burning hot because they know that the only guy that's got these records is me – Gene Anderson – and I'm promoting these records first for everybody.

Now other labels start to get me in. We get a label by the name of Enjoy, from a guy named Bobby Robinson (no relation to Joe and Sylvia). He sends us a record. Now, there were several small labels that was contacting us with records that were tryin' to rap, but they wasn't as strong as Joe's records. Joe Robinson and Sylvia Robinson had the hottest records of them all.

Then I get a call from Joe, he says, "Man, my son, he quit school. He don't wanna go to school no more, man. What's with that?" He was really upset. "That's my son, Joey Robinson. That was my baby boy."

I said, "Give him to me, I can talk to him."

Then when I started talking to him, his mind was on music. He started a group called Ferrari and the West Street Mob. They put out a record. And, the next thing you know, another record came out.

Sugar Hill came out with a song called, "Apache"–"Hunger, hunger, hunger!" Boy, I promoted that record then they came out with their album.

But that "Rapper's Delight" record was still hot! They was trying to figure out why they couldn't get their records on the charts–on the Billboard charts. Their record was the biggest record in the world.

So I said, "Joe, why don't you just cut it in half and make a 45 of it?"

He said, "I never even thought about it like that!"

I said, "Joe, cut it in half and make a 45 of it, and I'll get it put on the jukeboxes."

He sent us in about a thousand 45s on it edited down, and I took it to the jukebox people in St. Louis–their name was Rafey's.

Rafey was the old mafia-kinda guy that owned all the jukeboxes all the way through Missouri and Illinois. But he knew me because I had been selling him my own personal records for years, and he was a good friend of Skip's. So he took 100 records and put "Rapper's Delight" on 100 jukeboxes. The record took off again.

Now, somewhere along the line, even though they had more records out, this one record had gotten so big that they leased the record to Morris Levy.

Joe called me and told me about it on the phone, 'cause I'd gotten so close to Joe that everything he was doin' he was calling me, because I was sort of like I was under his wing, more or less. Because he liked the heart that I had, because I wasn't letting nothing stop me from promoting these records 'cause I was finally getting a paycheck from doing some stuff that I was born to do, 'cause I've still got to raise this kid.

So, Joe gives me the information that he's going to lease the record to Morris Levy, over to Roulette. Because the record had gotten so big that he couldn't handle it no more. He couldn't handle the manufacturing of the records or nothing. So, he gave the record to Morris Levy.

The record comes back out again on Roulette Records. It stayed out and it began to blow up through the roof on Roulette Records. It had a yellow label with dots around it.

So we didn't have the distribution of the record no more, because they were goin' to the big boys, 'cause it was on Roulette. But somewhere along the line, Joe made enough money and made enough noise that Sylvia insisted on Joe going back to get the record back from Morris Levy and putting it back out himself.

That's when they came out with the blue label with the horn of plenty around it, and that was the new Sugar Hill logo up until today.

And they re-released "Rapper's Delight" again, for the third time. It came from the red label, to the yellow label with Roulette, to the powder blue label with the horn of plenty that is now Sugar Hill Records.

Big-time Booking

Now, we are rollin', and Joe said, "Listen. I wanna have a worldwide concert with this rap stuff."

They'd never had a rap concert, ever. Joe came down and we booked the Kiel Auditorium in St. Louis. He brought in all the crew. He brought in Sequence. Everybody wanted to see Sequence—Cheryl the Pearl, Angie B, and Blondie. Everybody wanted to see 'em. Them girls had got the biggest record in the world by doing some P-Funk stuff on the rap for the first time.

And everybody wanted to see this guy Grandmaster Flash because his name had gotten so big after this lady, Blondie, had cut a record called "Rapture" and had mentioned his name in the record. And that made him, and rap music, more popular because she was a big pop artist. As a matter of fact, she was really a disco artist. And that meant that rappin' had gone to the mainstream. She did give rap a lot of help by mentioning his name in that song.

So, the bus finally pulled up. This guy named Harold was with them. Harold was the guy that really sent the records out, that wrote the words in red ink printing, "Rapper's Delight," that was on the original test white label.

Harold was just like Joe's right-hand man, and he made sure that everything was goin' straight. And he had those wild young fellas under control. And when the bus pulled up, I was so anxious to meet him that I didn't know what to do, man.

We had set up in-store promotions for him and stuff. So we went out to a store by the name of Peaches. It was a big warehouse-type record store, a big chain store. And I was taking him around the store, and the girls was just fightin' over 'em, they didn't know what to do. But the boys were so young and so green that they didn't have any idea what an autograph session in a record store was like.

So, I never will forget, the young fella named Master G walks up to me and said, "Mr. Anderson, what is an autograph?"

I said, "Why?!"

He said, "This girl keeps asking me for my autograph and I don't know what she's talkin' about."

I said, "Son, it's just your name. Put your name on it and give it to her."

Everybody cracked up, he went up and gave his name. It was just such a thrilling experience to see something that I had created in that area, to have done it myself and to have this much enthusiasm with all of the people that was around. They wanted to touch and meet and to be with the artists around me that I had made stars in my area.

And it was the first time that any rap stars had ever been in the area, because they had never had a rapper's tour before. This was the first rapper's tour.

The big record at that time was "Apache."

So that night we went to the Kiel Auditorium. Everybody was very excited and anxious. Jim Gates and them were stars over at WESL, that I flanked KATZ with, which was the powerhouse of the area, and all of the other stations—Magic 108 and whoever else was concerned.

The little itty bitty station in east St. Louis that was WESL was hosting the first ever rap show at the Kiel Auditorium in St. Louis. Man, that place was packed all the way to the rafters. I mean, there wasn't a seat left over. There was excitement in the air. No one had ever expected to see a rap tour or show ever in that area. They couldn't imagine there ever being one because there had never been one before!

Not only that, it was the first time I'd ever seen Joe

Robinson. He finally showed up. He had talked to me for a long time on the phone explaining to me what he wanted me to do, and he literally taught me the promotional record game over the telephone. We had talked daytime, nighttime, and he was telling me exactly what he wanted me to do. And I was listening to other people around me that really had known Joe from back in the day when he had first started with All Platinum. Like I said, Joe was like the Al Capone of the record business. If Joe said it, he meant it, and most of the time it was done just like he wanted it.

I was his boy. Somehow, along the way, he fell in love with the idea I had so much heart, I would never question him about what he'd asked me to do, and when he'd look up it was done just like he said, if not better. And the better I made Joe look, the better it made me look.

And so, the word got out on a national level that they got this young kid in St. Louis that's breaking all of Joe's records. He'd never miss one. So Joe was like extremely excited at the fact that he had made this monster promotion man out of me.

When he got there, the first thing he did when he saw me was he put a $100 bill in my hand and balled it up. I didn't know what it was and when I looked at it, it was a hundred dollar bill! I hadn't been handling too much money, so that was more than a welcomed sight.

He was excited because he had successfully got the first rap show together. He had all the stars in town. He had everybody in town wantin' to see him. The records was hot as a rocket, and it was going good for him and he said that I was one of the causes of things happening. Because he knew I didn't have no help and I had a lot of obstacles in my way because the music I was handling was so new—this rap music.

He explained to me his concerns at that particular time

was on his new artists like Sequence—these were three girls out of Columbia, South Carolina, who won a talent show, and his wife Sylvia Robinson had discovered them and brought them to Jersey and recorded them a record called, I think it was, "Funk You Up."

And the record exploded. It was a take-off of ones of the George Clinton P-Funk records. And it was Cheryl the Pearl, Angie B, and Blondie. They showed up in town. Them girls was so young and so country. I took 'em to a friend of mine by the name of Johnny Dunns and had their hair fixed so they could do the show. Joe gave me the money to take 'em down there. Everybody was so excited to meet 'em because they was talking about Sequence. They was the first girl rap group *ever*.

All I know is my name was ringing all over town—"Gene Anderson, Gene Anderson." That boy had fooled around there and created a monster with this rap music.

The disc jockeys liked it, and the streets, but the ones on the radio really weren't too particular about these records because they were so long and they only had one side on 'em and the other side was an instrumental.

And so, I used to have problems with all the big boys at them big stations about the records 'cause they kept telling me that this is the last one—there not gonna be no more hit records. And I knew better than that because Joe had them send me acetates on a lot of records that was coming out to see what I thought about them, and they were just as hot as the first one.

But nothing was as hot as "Rapper's Delight" because it had taken off three or four different times, as if it was a new record, and people were buying it and buying it and re-buying it, and guys was selling 'em out the trunk of their cars.

(l-to-r) Furious Five: Cowboy, Petey (son), Gene, Melle Mel, Scorpio

But they came along with this record called "Showdown." It was a showdown between Grandmaster Flash and the Furious Five and the Sugar Hill Gang. This record took off like you would not believe, 'cause it was both of the biggest names and groups of their time on one record. And everybody wanted to see Grandmaster Flash and the Furious Five with Melle Mel and Scorpio and Cowboy and Rahiem. Oh man, they was all superstars. They still were just first-record artists but there was nobody to complete with 'em because nobody had never seen none of these rap artists before.

They also had Joe's son, Joey. He had a group called the West Street Mob. They had a hit record called "Let's Dance, Make Your Body Move." It was a big record for them but it wasn't a big one yet to come.

Also we had a hot record called "Freedom." That was a big record for the Furious Five. So we had a very hot, young, and fresh show and all of the youngsters seemed like they knew it.

A lot of the old DJs and the old guys—they didn't want rap to happen. They were fighting every step of the way. But it was so huge, if you just mentioned it, somebody got excited.

The First Rap Concert

We finally got to the Kiel Auditorium and the show was about to start. A little bit before the show started, Wonder Mike has an asthma attack. He can't breathe. He's the star of the show; he's first guy to say "hip hop, hip hop!" of the Sugar Hill Gang. Nobody knew what to do. He can't breathe.

I grabs him up, puts him in my mother's car, and takes him to Barnes Hospital. I rushed him over there and tell them who he is, run past all the people in the emergency room. They give him an albuterol treatment. He couldn't breathe, he was about to go out it looked like, and I got him back to the show just in time for them to go on the stage.

I missed most of the show, but I understand that the people were so rowdy and got so crazy and excited and hyper about this rap show that they was all on the stage. The police were trying to get people off the stage.

And there was a big transvestite by the name of Buster. Everybody knew him from St. Louis. He was about 6'1" or 6'2", and he dressed in drag. He got up on the stage and we had to almost have him arrested to get him off the stage. Boy, he was just trying to get up there with the stars. It was funny today, but then it wasn't funny. They had the spotlight on him, and the more that they had the spotlight on him, the crazier he would get. And everybody knew him, they was hollerin', "Go, Buster! Go, Buster!" It was hilarious.

But anyway, we finally got him off the stage and Grandmaster Flash had done his record. They had done "Freedom." They had done "Happy Birthday." They had been on the road, so they went up to the dressing room and the Sugar Hill came on and they was setting the place on fire.

All of a sudden, it was time to do the big record between

the Sugar Hill Gang and Grandmaster Flash and the Furious Five, and it was called The Showdown. Everybody was anticipating and waiting for The Showdown.

They called them on the stage and there was no Furious Five. Everybody was saying, "Find 'em, find 'em. Gene, find 'em. Find 'em."

I looked all over for 'em. Something told me to go up to the dressing room. And I go up in the dressing room, all five of 'em, there they was in the dressing room. All five of them with a dressing room full of girls—everybody was butthole naked. The girls were naked, they're naked. I got my belt and started beating their ass saying, "Get up outta here and get up to the show!" They was laughing.

That's how rappers became the way that they look today, on the stage with no shirts. 'Cause they didn't have all their clothes on, 'cause they had to get out on the stage. They was running down the steps trying to put their pants on. I'm laughing, but I'm trying to get 'em to the stage to do the show. They got the show held up and a couple of 'em – Melle Mel, I believe, and maybe Cowboy – didn't have no shirts on and they went on the stage with no shirts, and they did "Showdown."

Man, they must have did the song ten minutes, fifteen minutes. They set the place on fire! And when they got through doing the song, they didn't go to the wings. They jumped off the edge of the stage and got down in the audience with the people.

It was so hilarious, 'cause I was young myself, I thought it was great to see them just so free 'cause all the show that had been stage shows in our area had always been conservative doo-wop singers or soul and stuff. And everybody was trying to be so cool. These boys was loose and like the guy next door, and they was having nothing but fun. And I was having fun with 'em, and the show was such a tremendous success. It was unbelievable.

And then, I understand it was the very first rap or hip-hop show *ever*.

Ridin' High

After the show was over, everybody went back to the hotel. Joe and I, we had a little meeting with Gates and all of the jocks that Gates had – Curtis Soul, Spiderman, Jockenstein, Randy OJ – all of the guys in St. Louis that was really rolling with the new youth thing. They was running with the P-Funk records and the Joe Robinson Hip Hop records. Joe took everybody out for a big dinner after the show.

So Joe tells me, he says, "Gene, take me around to some of the clubs so I can see what they're doin' and what they're playing."

It was 2 o'clock in the morning and, you know, St. Louis closed at 1:30, so I had to take him over to East St. Louis. So we got into, he had leased, a new Mercedes Benz and I had never ridden in a new Mercedes Benz before. So it was like, it was exciting to me, ya know? And to ride with Joe Robinson, too, man. Joe was a legend as far as I was concerned. And the world knew who he was. Joe had already been a millionaire two or three times, so Joe was very poised and very sharp he was a strong looking guy, real tall and handsome and people just loved him, man.

And he was the epitome of what they call "a player." Joe was just that, and he had that gangster image, so he had a love juice and he always had *too* much money. Sometimes a briefcase full of money.

So, we go over to East St. Louis. I took him to an after-hours joint. We had to go in through the back way, and they had a bunch of tall weeds as tall as we were but they had a pathway and you had to go through the pathway.

And Joe kept going to me, "Gene, do you know what you're doin'?"

And I'd say, "Yeah, Joe, come on. Follow me."

We walked through there, through this little pathway, and I knocked on the door and gave him the signal. I went, 'bam bam bam bam bam bam...' And somebody looked through a little sliding door and said, "Oh, it's Poo Poo Man, Gene Anderson."

They opened the door, and we went in, and as soon as we walked in the door they was playin' one of Joe's Hip Hop records, one of Joe's rap records. As soon as we walked in the door, it was playin' already, and he reached over and gave me another $100 bill.

He said, "Now, nobody do your job like you do it, Gene. 'Cause I didn't have to come here and see if they'll play my record. They was playin' 'em as soon as you were comin' in."

'Cause he knew I had been everywhere. I had been in every little rat hole and that for Sugar Hill Records. 'Cause he would always send me.

After he got the records, he would always send 'em to Skip. But Skip was selling the records. He was selling 100 copies, but Skip was selling the promos and the records that he was buying from Joe, and I would always get at least 10, 15, 20, 25 of 'em but I'd do something with the records so everybody knew that I work for Sugar Hill records and I had the hot records that nobody else had, and I had 'em first.

All the club owners in East St. Louis and all up in Illinois, Lovejoy, Brooklyn, all of the joints in St. Louis, they knew who I was. They was waiting for me to come in and bring them some new records, and I never had to pay for nothing. I never had to pay to get into the clubs, and they'd make sure that I was okay. I could get in the club, get out of the club, and everything was going fine.

Joe was just so excited at the fact that he knew that he could break a record in St. Louis first and didn't have to worry about if the record was going to be okay or not, because I could let him know in two or three days if what kind of record he had wasn't big enough or whatever. And man, my relationship with Joe began to grow and grow and grow, and all he would talk about was, "This kid down in St. Louis, Gene Anderson. Send it to him, send it to him."

He was taking care of me, real good.

Power Shift

Joe began to take more control of how he wanted me to function on his behalf. Skip and them was a little upset with me because my name had gotten so big. Tony and Skip seemed to always have a little scheme going on.

But somehow, Tony got sick. He went to the hospital and I think he had diabetes, and they cut off his toe. And we went to the hospital to see Tony, and not only did they cut off his toe—in less than two weeks Tony was *dead*.

Tony died in the hospital, and nobody could understand how that went down. And yet, that left Skip with no compadre to work against me. So Skip had to work with me because I was the lifeline of keeping Midwest Distributors open, because I was promoting all of the records.

Now, after the big concert with all of these new records that I was promoting that my name has been affiliated with 'em first, other record companies had started to contact Midwest and wanted to be a part of that.

Skip told them that I couldn't promote their records unless they would distribute them through Midwest. So he began to get records from different companies. Another name that popped up was Bobby Robinson. He had that company called Enjoy Records.

Then another company popped up named Streetwise Records. Streetwise Records was run by Adam Levy, who was Morris Levy's son, I believe. He started to come up with rap records. All of the people in New York, New Jersey, that was making rap records started sending them to Midwest Record Distributors.

I get the call from Mercury Records one day and they had a record by the name of "The Christmas Rap" by Kurtis

Blow. As I said, he was the first individual rap artist that had popped up, behind these groups. They gave the record to me during the Christmas holiday. I took the record and broke the record overnight at a club called the Regal Room with Dr. Jockenstein and them. Next thing I knew, it was Christmas time as I said and they send to him there for a promo gig at the Regal Room.

This kid was unbelievable. He was the first one that we'd ever seen spinning records backwards, scratchin' and dancin' and rappin', like a one-man gang. People couldn't believe their eyes.

To this day, Kurtis Blow and I – it's been over 40 years – are still the best of friends. And he thanked me for promoting his early records, which I promoted–the first one was the Christmas rap, one was callcd "Basketball," and one was called "These Are the Breaks."

"Break it up! Break it up! Break it up! Breakdown..." Boy, that was a huge record for this kid.

Then I got another record by the name of "Move to the Groove" on Enjoy.

Then, before you knew it, my name had gotten all over the country. I was going around to different cities now. I was going to Kansas City; I was going to Memphis, Tennessee; I was going to Chicago; I was going to Joliet; I was going to Detroit; I was going to Milwaukee, Wisconsin; I was going all over the midwest promoting these records by myself.

Joe bought me a car. Joe bought me a little red Sunbeam, two-seater. That was so I could go all over the midwest, go to the clubs and stuff, and could promote these records and would have no problem getting there.

I looked up one day and the car was sitting out in front of my daddy's caravan. We had a caravan by the name of International Hook-Up, and that's where all of the stars started to hang out by my daddy's club because they knew I was promoting these records. And all of the disc jockeys was coming up there to pick up a copy of these records, because I always had 'em first.

It had gotten to a point where I didn't even want this much money—they'd send me 100, 200, 300 records and I could get my own money.

They had a lady that worked up at Sugar Hill by the name of Agnes. Agnes became a very good friend of mine, and between her and Joey and Joe, they would always send me 100 or 200 of the new records to my daddy's club, they knew I had the hookup, because they knew Skip was not giving me the records that they were sending down there to Midwest Record Distributors for me to work with. So I would have more records to promote, and I could get the records saturated faster.

I had gotten to the point where I put a new record on and watched the dancefloor. If I got five people to dance, I knew it was a mediocre record. But if I got a dancefloor full, I knew that was a million seller, every time. So I would tell them right away the kind of record that they had. My name had gotten so big that people was calling me from everywhere.

One day, I get a call from a guy, again from Mercury records. He got a record, he said, "This record has been out for months," and it hadn't done nothing. He heard about me, he said, "I'll tell ya what I'll do. I'll send you a few hundred dollars and if the record turns gold I'll give you the gold record on it, if you can break this record."

And the record was "Bounce, Rock, Skate, Roll" by Vaughan Mason & Crew. I took that record, I think he sent me about 25 or 30 of 'em. I took that record to all of the skating rinks around Illinois, St. Lewis, and Alton, and I broke the record right there in St. Louis—Bounce, Rock, Skate, Roll.

I got to keep the gold record, and I've still got the gold record now. When it came into the office, Skip almost had a hemorrhage. It broke his heart for me to get the gold record.

Skip had claimed to be the owner of the distributor because Mr. Goldman had retired, because he was so old he just couldn't take it no more. And he left the distributor all to Skip. I had a little leverage when Mr. Goldman was around, but it was no longer him in charge.

Skip, his two daughters, and his wife had commandeered the whole distributor. So now I don't even have an office no more, I'm just about a visitor in the place because they was trying to take all the money. I wasn't getting no more money from out of there, because he knew I was making money in the streets. But I still was supposed to be getting a regular salary because I was promoting all their records, too.

At this point, I'm really having problems with Skip, so I'm trying to do things on my own and I've still got to take care of this kid, so the only thing I could think of was to call Joe and tell Joe that I was in a panicked situation down here.

The Record Hustler

Joe was about to have a big affair up there at Sugar Hill Records for a celebration on the triple platinum album for "Rappers Delight." So he sent for me and Jim Gates to fly up there to New Jersey at Sugar Hill, in order for us to be in the affair. To show me off to everybody – as the youngster that had broke his records for him and got all this stuff started – would give me a little juice to be able to get more things done on my end.

Picture of original Sugar Hill Gang taken by Gene Anderson l-to-r): Big Bank Hank; Wonder Mike; Master G

And, as I said earlier–the better I made Joe look, the better it made me look. And the better he made me look, the better it made him look. So it was one of those situations.

We finally got to New Jersey. Joe took me to dinner. I never will forget it and we went to a place where I had my first lobster. The lobster was so big that the lobster was bigger than the plate. I think Joe paid $300 for this lobster.

The reason that I remember it so well is that I would get at him and say, "Joe, I can't believe you paid two to three hundred dollars for eating lobster. You have to know you could give me two-three-hundred in my pocket!" He would die laughing when I'd start with that. I'd always come at him with that when I was tryin' to get some money out of Joe, 'cause Joe was like my daddy. He loved me.

As a matter of fact, him and Ms. Sylvia—she was a *queen*. She was an unbelievably wonderful and brilliant person. When I met her, I always had known who she was because I was a big fan of hers when I was a youngster lookin' at her and a guy named Mickey on television. They had a record called, "Love is Strange."

I used to see them on the Alan Freed show on television and I thought that she was one of the most beautiful women in the whole wide world. And she was. But she was even more beautiful on the inside than she was outside. She was so smart and she just fell in love with me as soon as she saw me. She said, "Joe, we've got to do something with this kid."

She was always on my side. If I ever needed something and Joe would be stubborn about it, she would always be there for me. God bless her forever and ever.

When I got to New Jersey, I knew that I was on my way to doing something that was unimaginable, as far as my prior career was concerned, because I really wasn't a promoter. Joe made me a promoter. And between Skip and them, through survival, I became a very knowledgeable record promoter. As a star, I had kind of petered off because, like I said, I had to give up all of that in order to try and raise my son by myself.

Eventually I got a chance to meet all of Joe's sons. I got a chance to meet Leland, and I got a chance to meet the other little brother. And me and Joey was already tight. I never will forget, I was in one of the offices over there at Sugar Hill Records, and Joey played me a *cassette*.

A cassette was the thing that they had, back in the day, when everybody had a boom box. And on that first cassette he had was a song by the group Soul Sonic Force, and the name of the song was "Planet Rock."

He told me, he said, "Gene, I've been trying to get 'em to sign this group, 'cause this is gonna be a big record."

He played the tape for me and I could never believe what I heard. It was a new sound, with a new beat. But he said Joe didn't want the group because he had already signed so many groups, had so many records, and all of 'em were basically successful. So he didn't have no room for another group.

There was a guy that I had already met at a convention, and he was a guy that was sort of hanging around Sugar Hill—his name was Tom Silverman. He started a record company by the name of Tommy Boy Records.

He signed Soul Sonic Force, along with some other stuff that Joe didn't want and Bobby Robinson didn't want, and he just stayed around and hung around and just picked up all he could, and the game that he got from them. And it ended up being one of the biggest record companies in the world.

His and my relationship was very strong, and I would meet him later on in life in conventions. I'll get around to that shortly.

Joe's son, Leland, used to be my boy. He would take me around and we'd go all around New Jersey and stuff. And he always carried a blackjack or something. I asked him why and he said, "These are tough gangsters in this town, and I'm not gonna let nobody bother you or me." And I always laughed at that because I was a Vietnam Veteran. If anything, I could take care of him, but it always looked like he was takin' care of me. That was my boy, I loved him so much.

I ran into Melle Mel. He was goin' through the parking lot and he spotted me, and we got to talkin' and hugging each other. Me and him have always been very close, and we still are close. And he told me, he said, "Mr. Anderson, you know what? I'm gonna be one of the biggest rappers in the world one day."

"Well I hope so, son," I said, "'Cause you got all the potential in the world."

"Yeah," he said, "We're gonna be bigger than the Sugar Hill Gang."

I said to myself, *that'd have to be awful big*, 'cause that was the biggest group in the world at the time. But he had so much confidence, and so much conviction in his voice. I listened to what he said and sure enough, in time, Melle Mel became the number one rapper in the whole wide world.

So, as time went on, we went back over to Joe's house. Joe had one of the most magnificent houses that, at that time, I'd ever seen. It was *huge*. And he said – his exact words – he said, "Gene, rich white folks have this all the time. It ain't nothing new. I just got it for now." I never forgot that, because it let me know that it's possible that I could have something like that, especially back in those days.

Joe had one of those big 'ol huge projection televisions, that was bigger than the whole wall on one side of the room. And he had a wicker room–a room that had nothing but wicker furniture in it.

"Man," he said, "You see that room, Gene."

I said, "Yeah."

He said, "Ain't nobody been in that room for five years. That room just be sittin' there."

We busted out laughin'. And I can't forget that because it was things I hadn't seen that Joe was showing me. He always wanted to show me something that could enhance my desire for bigger and better things. Because Joe really did love me, and he wanted me to be something special, 'cause he knew I had something that was a little unique and different from a guy that was just a hustler—I was a record hustler.

From All Platinum to Sugar Hill

So he asked me to go up to the office the next day and, I was sittin' there, he had a big meeting. And there was all the old pros that I had heard about as record promoters. All of the big boys: he had the Mad Hatter; he had Spiderman; he had another old gansta', Joe Medlin; Red Forbes had came back.

As a matter of fact, Red Forbes was Joe's personal partner that came through the ranks with him and had been with him through All Platinum and all of the major stuff that he had done. But somewhere along the line, Joe and Red had had a falling out before he came up with Sugar Hill Records and all of that. That's why Joe had to find somebody to do his promotions for him. That's why he found *me*—because he didn't have Red Forbes.

But Joe had gotten so huge and so big that him and Red, well Red wasn't crazy. Red knew that it was best to get back with Joe because Joe was the man that was making things happen in the record industry. He had changed the whole industry with these 12-inch records.

At this point in time every promoter, from New York to Mississippi, was lookin' forward to workin' for Joe. Joe hired everybody that he could get to promote and sell these records. Joe did something in the record industry that had never been done in record history. Joe sold the first rap records over what then was called the "Iron Curtain" over in Russia. They didn't have no way of exchanging the money because Russia had currency called rubles. Rubles were not accepted in the United States at that time, I understand. And Joe had sold so many records over in the Soviet Union that he had to figure out how to get his money. And he explained to me how he made it happen.

He took the rubles that they paid him for distribution, behind the Iron Curtain, and bought lumber. Russian wood–*lumber*. Then he sold the lumber over to Canada, got the Canadians to pay him in Canadian money, and exchanged the Canadian money into American money. This is how he made a million dollars in just manipulating currencies from over in the Soviet Union. That's when there was no trading going on between the Soviet blocs and the Americans. I always looked at that as being a stroke of true genius, how he was able to pull that off.

Joe would always tell me things like that in order for me to be able to see how I could be able to use the wisdom and the knowledge that he had to better myself. Because he always wanted me to do better and always wanted me to have bigger things in life and to dream bigger.

Because he knew I had something special inside of me, because the way I took those records from nothin', from nowhere, and made them so sought after around the world probably. Because most of them all got started in St. Louis. If the record was big in St. Louis, it went big around the world. If it didn't really happen in St. Louis, they pay no attention, they gave up on it.

Most of the record industry was watchin' Sugar Hill Records now, because Joe was already a super name in the record industry from owning All Platinum, because he had big stars over there.

Remember, the reason why he got rid of that name, All Platinum, and went to Sugar Hill Records was because he was in that law suit with a group called The Moments. He had to give up doing any business under the banner of All Platinum. That is why Sugar Hill Records was born.

Rocking the Universal Suite

Shortly after that, we went to a convention in Atlanta, Georgia, called Jack the Rapper at the Peachtree Plaza. It was owned by a guy by the name of Jack Gibson and they called him Jack the Rapper.

Everybody wanted to be affiliated with Jack the Rapper back in the day because he would give you a shot. He was like our Billboard Magazine.

He was the poor man's convention and the independent's convention and he was everybody's friend. We loved him, and that's where you could meet all the big boys. So, when I showed up down there I went with all of our crew. We had those jackets on, WESL jackets, and we had all of the different colors. Jim Gates took all the DJs down to Jack the Rapper.

We all looked like we was in a motorcycle gang more or less but we was all sharp and we was organized all like brothers, and we set a trend amongst all of the national Disc Jockeys that these guys in St. Louis they got a bond going on and everybody wanted to hang out with *us*!

I met a lot of big time guys, I met my man that I really love named Mr. Max Kid. He had his own independent label from out of Washington, D.C., but he had a record called "We Need Some Money" by Chuck Brown.

He started the go-go records and I used to help him with those records because we had Trouble Funk which he once owned. Trouble Funk was owned by Turbo which belonged to Joe and at first that didn't take off for him before he came up with Sugar Hill so we got real tight. I had cut a record over there with a friend of mine by the name of Eddie Fisher by the name of "Give Up the Poo Poo." That's how I really got a chance to jump start my singing career again with this crazy record, "Give Up the Poo Poo."

I had also cut a record for Eddie Fisher by the name of "The Gigolo" and I had those records in my pouch, and I had some more Sugar Hill records, and so we was going around and he had sent me a test pressin' on a record called "The Message" by Melle Mel and the Furious Five, him and Duke Bootee, so when we got to the convention we ran into our old friend, George Clinton.

George Clinton had a suite upstairs where he was promoting his record that the record company had blackballed him and was trying to hold him down because George was real swift. He had five or six different record labels that he was on with one big group which he gave them different names like The Funkadelics, The Parliaments, The Bride of Funkenstein, The Horny Horns, The Sweatbands—all these different groups and The Parlettes, and he had a first George Clinton record which was called "Atomic Dog."

So, he had a suite and everybody wanted to see George because George was flying high at that time, but he didn't have no hot hit record and he was trying to make a record out of "Atomic Dog." So, we went up to his suite, me and Jockenstein and Jim Gates—we all went up to George Clinton's suite so we showed the record "The Message" to George and he played it and man, he fell in love with the record!

"Man, this is phenomenal!" he said, "Give me a copy of it."

I had a couple of copies so I gave him a copy.

He said "I ain't playing nothing in my suite the whole week but Atomic Dog and The Message!"

George started grinding, and everybody was coming up

to his suite and they was coming out of the suite talking about, "Man did you hear that record 'The Message?' Did you hear that record 'Atomic Dog?' Did you hear that record 'The Message?' Did you hear that record 'Atomic Dog?'"

The whole convention, they had all kinds of records that was going on but they was only thinkin' about those two records. They was the talk of the whole convention.

Plus I was trying to push that "Give Up the Poo Poo" and we had just gotten some bumper stickers, which we were sticking on everything – *Give up the Poo Poo* – and we had one by "The Gigolo." We had "The Message" and I had about five, six or seven copies of it, and I was sneaking it in every suite playing it.

So, we went down to Warner Brothers. Their chief promotion man at that time was an ex DJ from St. Louis by the name of Donny "Soul Finger" Brooks. He was running things down there and there was an old slick guy by the name of Walt Baby Love—a White boy that everybody loved because he had all of the cocaine. He had all of the payola; he had everything to work with because they had gave him everything to work with.

Come to find out, he was working for Tommy Boy at that time. Tommy Boy was pushing a gang of different rap records, and he was doing alright with them. But when I ran into Walt Baby Love, ya know, he said, "What you working?"

"I'm working 'The Message' ," I said, "I'm working 'Give up the Poo Poo' , I'm working 'The Gigolo' ."

And he said, "Well wait a minute."

I said "What you working?"

"Well I got this record and that record," he said, "but I got a record over here."

"Hey man," I looked in his bag and said, "Here's a record on this group called Soul Sonic Force."

"I ain't doing nothing with that record, man," he said, "I don't like that record."

I say, "Hey man, that's my friend's record. Let me see it."

He gave me a copy, so I went over to Donny Brooks and I said, "This is a smash hit record."

He said, "You really think so?"

"Listen, man, Donny Brooks," I said, "Do me a favor."

He was running the Warner Bros. party. All of the people were dancing to all of the Warner Bros. records and they was givin' away all kinds of stuff. They were going in the back room and doing a little tricky slick shit and I was in the clique because everybody wanted to talk to me—because I was the boy that had put the nucleus of Sugar Hill on the map!

So I asked him, I said, "Donny Brooks, do me a favor. Play this record for me, man, Soul Sonic Force's 'Planet Rock'."

He said "Man, I don't know. This is Warner Brothers' suite."

I said, "Come on Donny. Do that for me, man."

And all of the St. Louis boys said, "Hey man!"

They was all behind me because I had all of the juice, plus Jordan gave me "Planet Money." Joey Jr. was down there and he was backing my play with everything that I needed. Plus I got this hot hit record "The Message" and I'm circulating it around down there.

So Donny said, "Okay, I'll give you one spin."

He played the "Planet Rock...Rock...Rock...to the Planet Rock..." and *everybody* in the party went to the roof! They went Berserk! And boy, he had to play it again and again and, before you know it, the record had busted out at Jack the Rappers, down at Peachtree Plaza in Atlanta, Georgia!

So my friend Big Ralph, Big Boy, he brought in a bunch of the "Give Up The Poo Poo" and "The Gigolo" records for me, 'cause he had a ride to get down there. And he brought a huge, big ol' box of about 400 to 500 bumper stickers–"Give Up The Poo Poo" bumper stickers.

So we went upstairs, on the top floor, because there was a big balcony that looked down into the lobby where everybody was millin' around. And we took those bumper stickers and threw 'em over the top of the rail, and they floated all over the place.

People were saying, "Look at all of them!"

They was lookin' up and they was amazed, and it took 'em forever to hit down on the ground floor. Man, we almost beat 'em downstairs on the elevator before they all hit the floor. And man, people was grabbin' 'em and they were laughing at the "Give Up The Poo Poo" and "The Gigolo" bumper stickers.

The people running the convention was goin' crazy. The people that owned the hotel was upset because they were saying that it could've been a hazard to people, throwing stuff up over the balcony.

All it was was just the introduction to a thousand people throwing shit over the balcony. All day long, all through the convention, people was throwing stuff over the balcony. They was throwin' bloomers over the balcony that had record names on 'em. They was throwin' bubble gum. They was throwin' all kinds of stuff over the balcony that had names on 'em.

That's where my boy named Chuck Brown had a record called, "Money." They had a bunch of fake money that had his name on it, and Max Kid went up to the top and throwed about 5 or 600 of them over there.

By that time everybody was upset they was trying to find who was this guy Poo Poo Man that's started all this stuff being thrown over there. They weren't trying to get the big name guys that was doin' it. They was tryin' to get me.

I was hiding, laughing my ass off.

Joe Robinson finally showed up, and when he heard that I had been throwin' those stickers over the balcony he almost fainted he laughed so hard. He said, "That's my boy! He's doin' his thing."

'Cause he knew that the better I was making myself look down there, the better I'd have a chance to promote some more Sugar Hill records. I was building up my reputation as a force to be dealt with in promoting records. When I ran into Joe, the first thing he did was sneak 2 or 3 hundred dollar bills in my pocket and tell me, "Go get 'em, tiger."

That's why I love Joe so much. No matter what I did, he would take me to the side and say, "Hey Poo Poo, are you right with this? Are your ears right with this?" About 99 percent of the time he'd stand behind me no matter what.

Boy, I was rollin' like you wouldn't believe. Everybody was talkin' about me down there—me, Big Ralph, Dr. Jockenstein, and all those WESL boys. We had took that convention and ran off with it.

Basically, we was all hanging out in the George Clinton's suite. It was jam packed, 24 hours, and when I took Joey Jr. up there, he saw that they was playin' "The Message." Boy, he was so happy to know the dude, man.

I said, "Listen Joey, I got an idea for you."

He said, "What is it?"

I said, "Man, you know, I saw a dance down in Biloxi, Mississippi. It was guys by the name of Shaba Doo and them. They was doin' a dance called the *breakdance*."

And I told him, I said, "They're spinning on their head, spinnin' on their backs."

He said, "Yeah?!"

I said, "Listen, you oughta cut a record about the breakdance."

He said, "Imma think about that."

Little did I know, that later on he'd cut a big, huge record called "Breakdance Electric Boogie" by his group, the West Street Mob.

So, as the convention went on, we partied and did our lil' thang. I went back up to Joey's suite on the last day of the convention. I ran into a guy by the name of Ramone who was one of George's road managers at that time. He was in the P-Funk entourage and he was kind of handling and running things for George. The convention just about over and I say, "Ramone, gimme that damn record 'Atomic Dog', man."

He said, "We ain't got but a cassette left on it, man."

I said, "Well gimme the cassette."

He gave me a look, he said, "You know that goes into the boomboxes?"

I took the cassette, put it in my pocket, sneaked out the party with it. We finally left and I took it home to St. Louis. I took it to WESL to Dr. Jockenstein.

I said, "Jock! I got the cassette to 'Atomic Dog'."

He said, "No!"

I said, "Yeah I've got the cassette to 'Atomic Dog', man."

He took it, him and Jim Gates, and put the cassette on a radio cassette that they use to put commercials on at WESL. They stuck it in there and played "Atomic Dog" back to back to back to back. Then that night we went to Regal Room. He brought the cassette to Regal Room and a boombox, hooked it up to broadcast through the microphone and played it some more. Before you knew it, everybody in town was looking for "The Message" and they was looking for "Atomic Dog." We had done broke that record.

And Capital Records – I think it was Capital Records – they was upset because they was trying to hold George down and the record done busted open. The record had been out, I don't know how long. But now the whole wide world was callin' for "Atomic Dog" and "The Message."

Records to Die For

Next Joe said, "Listen, go to Chicago. I want you to take this record that you've got left to Pervis Spann at WVON and I want you to go and see Lee Michaels and give him this money so he'll play 'The Message.'"

"Cool," I said, so I jumped in my car that night and went down to Chicago, Illinois.

Soon as I got to town, it must have been 10 or 11 o'clock, I was driving to a club I used to sing in a long time ago. They had a disc jockey that was spinnin' records and the junk was jam packed. It called the Blue Orchid.

I gave him my little speil at the door. I told 'em I work for Sugar Hill Records, and I had this brand new Sugar Hill record that I wanted to give to the disc jockey to play. And they was up on that, because everybody was looking for a Sugar Hill Record. They didn't care what the name was on it—if it said Sugar Hill, they wanted it.

So they let me in, and I went over to the DJ and said, "Hey man, my name is Gene Anderson. I'm with Sugar Hill Records. I got this brand new record called 'The Message'. Could you give it a couple spins and see what it's like?"

He said, "Yeah man, give it here for a minute."

He put it in put the headphones to his head, he spin it, (zzzzzooooop!). All of a sudden he heard it and his ears perked up, he said, "Hell yeah! I'll play this, man."

So I'm feelin' good. I'm thinking, *Yeah man, I'm gonna break this record in Chicago in this big club, with all these people in here.*

He put the record on... "It's like a jungle sometimes. It makes me wonder. how I keep from goin' under."

Boy, the dance floor got jam packed immediately, and

they rocked and partied 'til the last note. He takes the record and (*eeeeek*) backs it up, and plays it again. The people was goin' crazy.

I said, "Yeah, man!"

They he went back and put on the "Rapper's Delight," then he put on some old Sugar Hill stuff. He just went Sugar Hill crazy. Then he went back and put "The Message" on again.

I said, "Man, I've got to go. I've got to get back to the radio station 'cause Pervis Spann comes on the air at midnight on WVON."

That was the purpose of me coming to Chicago, because Joe had sent me to see Pervis first.

So, I said, "Man, I've gotta go, gimme me record."

He said, "Nigga, I ain't giving you shit."

I said, "What?! What a minute man... That's the only record I got. I've got just one copy. I've got to get my record back and go down to the radio station."

He said, "Man, we ain't giving you shit. We're gonna keep this mother fuckin' record."

I said, "No man, don't do that bro."

He pulled out his *pistol* and pointed it at me.

He said, "Only way you're gonna get that record is to get past this pistol, mother fucker. Now get up on out of here."

I said, "Man, don't be like that... Hey bro, it ain't that busy, it ain't that serious, so forget it."

So, I'm kind of milling around now, I'm thinking, *What the fuck am I gonna do? I got out here and this son of a bitch fell in love with this record, took this record, talked about killin' me over the damn record!* And I knew Joe's gonna be upset because I wasn't supposed to stop in no club. I was supposed to go straight to Pervis Spann and then stop in the morning to give the money to Lee Michaels. And I flew in there and tried to do things on my own, took his record into a club and into the streets. The record was hot as a firecracker.

So the DJ finally turned his head for a second. When he turned his head I snatched the record up, put it under my coat, and slid out the door.

I ran down the block and jumped into my little red car that Joe had bought me. I made a U-Turn and, when I made the U-Turn going back past the club, the DJ and his brother were standing outside – this is the truth – with their pistols in their hand looking up and down the street.

I rolled the window down and I hollered out the window, "HI-YO, SILVER, AWAY!"

I burned rubber and got away, laughing my ass off. I know I've got a big record now 'cause these thugs wanna kill me over the damn record.

So I finally made it over to the radio station. It's too early, and Pervis ain't there. So I get in the car, I ride down to another joint called the Shiba.

The Shiba was a big, upscale disco that had two DJs spinning at the same time, back to back. That had a big glass separatin' the two different rooms—on one side of the room you couldn't hear what the other side was playin'.

So I went inside, I told 'em, said, "Hey man, I've got a brand new record by Grandmaster Flash called, 'The Message'. Could you give it a spin? I've tested the record out already."

He said, "Man, yeah, I'll play everything for Sugar Hill."

So I gave one of DJs the record and he put it on... "It's like a jungle sometimes, it makes you wonder..."

Man, the dance floor got packed immediately, and the people went crazy about it. Then I took the record and put it on the *other* side, for the other side's DJ to play it. They played it over there, and it was the same thing.

We must have switched the record back at least two or three times that night, on both sides of the DJ booth. 'Cause, like I said, on one side you couldn't hear what they was playin' on the other side, 'cause it was a two-sided club.

I took the record then I finally get over to Pervis Spann. Pervis Spann—he loved me. He was my man. You gotta go to the restaurant with him and eat some chili; you've gotta do whatever left he says 'cause he was the *man* in Chicago at that time. All the other stations wouldn't play it, but Pervis Spann would play it.

He didn't come on until midnight, but everybody listened to Pervis Spann. He could break more records than anybody in the city of Chicago. Even the big station, WGCI, couldn't break a record no better than Pervis Spann. So Pervis Spann was Joe's man, he was Mitchell's man, he was my man. And any artist that was struggling and tryin' to come up, Pervis Spann would give you a shot, the blues man. If you has a hit record, it would be big in the town of Chicago, from that little station—WVON.

It has once belonged to the Chess brothers, including Leonard Chess. They started that station back in the days of the early Rock 'n' Roll like Chuck Berry and Muddy Waters and all that. They had the station when E. Rodney Jones was the man that dictated what happened all over the United States—him and Lucky Cordell and Tom Joyner and Bill "Butterball" Crane and Don Cornelius.

Not only that, one day I was in there and I met Jessie Owens who was the sports announcer for the station. Jessie Owens was walking history to me. I was overwhelmed when I met him. He took me to lunch once over there—Wow!

But Pervis Spann ended up buying the station from the Chess brothers and was the first Black owner of a radio station in Chicago. He gave everybody an opportunity to be a star. That's why so many stars came through that station. Tyrone Davis came through that station. Johnny Taylor came through that station.

He was the blues man—Pervis Spann. I love him.

So, that morning I went over to the radio station, saw Lee Michaels, and gave him the money. Lee didn't want to take the money, 'cause they'd already given him money for something else.

Lee was sayin', "Wait a minute, man, he already gave us the money."

"Hey man, Joe sent me with the money," I said, "That's it, that's all."

I gave him the money, got up out of there, and headed back to St. Louis.

When I get back to St. Louis, I'm hanging out a place downtown called Touch of Class that was owned by Big Time Frank. That was the headquarters for one of the spots that WESL's DJs used to hang out.

Dr. Jockenstein was the resident jockey down there, and him and Randy OJ. Me and Ralph Big Boy Little were hangin' out down there, and that's when I ran into a friend of mine by the name of Michael Williams, who was the Editor of the tabloid newspaper called the *St. Louis Sentinel*.

He said, "Gene, ya know what? Your name is ringing all over town. How would you like to get with my newspaper?"

I said, "Man, I don't know nothing about no newspapers."

He said, "Listen—we want you to be the entertainment editor of the *Sentinel* newspaper, because we ain't got nobody else out there in the streets that knows everything and knows how to get around this town. And we can give you the credentials so you can get in anywhere, do anything."

I said, "Well, let me think about it, Mike. Let me see what Skip and them have got to say about this."

So I go back and talk to Skip and them, and Skip said, "Hey, Gene. This would be a good time to get something started where you can report on some of these records that are in our distributorship."

Then I talked to Joe about it and he said, "Hey, man. That's a good idea. 'Cause you can get a chance to show everybody our records and talk about what's goin' on in your record promotions in the newspaper, and everybody reads the newspaper."

I went back to Mike Williams and I took the job.

I said, "Hey, Mike, I don't know how to do this thing."

He said, "Listen, all you'll do is just talk in a tape recorder, bring it to me, and I'll get my girl to transcribe it. We'll print it out, and you just take pictures if you'd like, and we'll put your articles out as the entertainment editor of the Sentinel Newspaper."

That's how I got the chance to take us all national. The first article I put out, I talked about the Sugar Hill Gang and I talked about "The Message". I talked about all the stuff I had seen. I took pictures of all the nightclubs.

I started goin' around to all the nightclubs and taking pictures, and as I was taking pictures I was taking Sugar Hill records and all of the rap records that I was getting – 'cause I didn't have nothing but rap records – and putting 'em in the newspaper. I would take pictures of people dancing and stuff and send 'em back to Joe. Joe would be so excited.

Then, I was talking to Tom Silverman and all the rest of the guys out there. They were sending me money and everything. Skip was getting jealous.

Skip said, "Hey man, why don't you split the money with us?"

I said, "Man, Skip, you've gone and took the whole distributor, now I've gotta split the money?"

'Cause they was sending the money, a lot of it, in to the office for me giving them favors in the newspaper.

So Skip gave me an idea. He said, "I'll tell you what then.

Here's what you can do to help us all... Why don't you start a record chart?"

I said, "A record chart?"

At that time record charts, in the radio stations and the record shops and all of those different outlets, were very important because people would read a lot and be able to know what the hit records were and what position they were in before they go to the store and purchase their records.

So, I started the "International Hook-Up" record chart.

I started putting in records that was hot in the streets, that was coordinating with the radio stations. I had "Pick Hits of the Week" and "Special Spins of the Week," all kinds of different stuff like that. And I'd always put two or three Sugar Hill records in there that was comin' up, and I would always make the Sugar Hill records #1 on the record chart.

Now people started calling me from across the country, saying, "Hey man, we know you've got this record chart in this newspaper." And it was making some difference because I was hooked up with all the record distributors in the one-stop shop and the mom-and-pop shops, talking with them about the records they was sellin'. That was making them some money, and keepin' it fresh in the newspaper that was sent out *around the world*.

I started making some money with that, then Joe sent me out on a record call—"Breakdance Electric Boogie". Joey had finally cut the record, and the record had took off a little bit in New York. So I took the record and I started to promote it, and the record began to get bigger and bigger.

Then he told me to take the record to Chicago. I took the record to Graham Armstrong. Graham Armstrong told me, he said, "Gene Anderson, I'm not playin' no more rap records because rap is gonna die. It ain't gonna last no longer."

"Graham, you've got to be crazy," I said, "This is gonna be

the biggest record in the world. This is the biggest dance since the Charleston and the Twist."

He said, "Man, I don't believe it. It's just another fluke."

"Okay," I said, and I took the record back to WVON. They stuck it down and before you know it the record was hot as a rocket.

So, to make a long story short, I'll have to skip over somethin'. We went to the BRE (Black Radio Exclusive) Conventions later on that year, and I was sittin' in the auditorium waiting for the main show. And who walks over to me, it was Graham Armstrong.

He said, "Gene, I've come over here to apologize to you."

I said, "Whatchu talkin' 'bout, Graham?"

He said, "Man..."

He reached into his back pocket and pulled out a copy of *Time* magazine and on the front cover was breakdancers. "I never would've dreamed this would happen," he said, "I wanted to be man enough to come and apologize to you, 'cause you brought it to me first and I could've been first."

All I knew was that, from that minute on, I felt like Superman. I knew that if Graham had come over to talk to me like that, then everyone was talkin' about me because I had told everyone that I could see or talk to and catch up with about that record, "Breakdance Electric Boogie".

Nobody had wanted to play it, except those that I had forced to play it. Matter of fact, I went to KATZ and they had a Program Director at that time by the name of AJ Kemp. He was the Program Director from out of Philadelphia. He wasn't giving nobody from St. Louis any kind of play. He was tryin' to play hardball with everybody living.

So I took the record over to him – "Breakdance Electric Boogie" – and he said, "Man I'm not gonna play no rap records. We ain't playin' no more rap records, 'cause rap records ain't gonna work no more, man. We're through with that. I'm playin' nothing but stuff out of Philadelphia."

"Man, do you know what? This is all I got is rap records!" I said, "I got a family to take care of, man, and you mean. You're just gonna turn my records down on the stint that you just don't want to play my records 'cause you're gonna play all Philadelphia records? I'll tell you what then, punk."

I pulled my gun out.

He fell back on the desk and said, "Man, wait! What're you doin' this for?"

"Listen, man," I said, "All I've got is rap records, so you're gonna play this record. Otherwise you're gonna have a problem with me."

I shut the door on us both. I was desperate 'cause my kid had caught a terrible cold. I was pressed, didn't have much money. I was pressed, tryin' to get shit together, and I wasn't gonna let him just tell me nothing like the reason why he wasn't gonna play the record.

I said, "It's war then, motha fucka."

"I'll tell you what I'll do," he said, "I'll play the instrumental side of it."

I said, "What the fuck you play the instrumental side for? If that's the case, it's a half of one and I've still got this pistol."

He said, "Okay, I'll play the record. I'll play the record."

'Cause I just spooked him. I walked out the door and he got on the phone and called Joe.

He said, "Joe, this little crazy motha fucka you got – Gene Anderson – he came in to threaten me. He pulled out a pistol on me, man, about this fuckin' record."

Joe said, "Listen, man. Gene Anderson is his own man and whatever he says and he does, I'm behind him. So don't call me with that shit..." and hung up in his face.

Before you knew it, that record was singin' up and down the radio like you wouldn't believe. The word got out across the country that Gene Anderson went and pulled a pistol out on a DJ up there in the radio station and made him play a Sugar Hill record.

Boy, the word got out and everybody in the country was callin' me laughing their ass off, saying, "Joe, you got the right one, baby."

The Rise to the Top

There are various times and situations that I still remember of my adventures at Sugar Hill.

I remember once Joe sent for me to come to New York to hear some of the new records that they was about to release prior to releasing them. I got off the plane. Joey came and got me in a little powder blue, 2-seater Mercedes convertible. I thought that was the sharpest little car. He was smart and smooth-moving, and everybody knew Joey. He was like he was in a parade all the time. He was always waving out of the car for somebody, reaching out of the car to help somebody.

Everyday, Joey would take me through the projects and through all kinda places, to upscale clubs and stuff and meet people. Joey was a very friendly, outward youngster, but he was super smart. Joe was grooming him to be the boss to take over all of his life. He really respected and loved me because he knew I knew about this record business, and he knew that a lot of stuff that happened in that company, I was informed on it and I had an opinion. He would always come to me for my opinion about different situations and certain things in the record business because if I didn't know, I would always go and find out and get back to him about it. We had a bond of real friendship.

So, he took me around to a studio one day and Scorpio was cutting a record called "Scorpio", and it was the first record I'd ever heard with that type of electronic voice on it – other than "Planet Rock" – but it was a different type of voice. I couldn't understand what it was he was trying to show with that record, but it was so advanced that no one had ever heard that type of voice.

Eventually, I got a hold of that record called "Scorpio". When I took that record to the streets, people went berserk over the record. The record was number one in my markets almost overnight. They was going to the store and storming the store, tryin' to buy that record, "Scorpio". Everybody wanted to see him 'cause I think his name was Mr. Ness first, but he had changed his name to Scorpio after that record or prior to that record. But, anyway, everybody wanted to see him do that song, "Scorpio." No one knew how he had done this voice, and he was showing me the machine that he was using to put that voice on there, and to this day, that is still one of the most unique, electronic-sounding-voice records of all time. As a matter of fact, it was groundbreaking, and I gotta give him credit. He came up with that.

Then, as a matter of fact, I remember Grandmaster Flash had come up with a record called "The Wheels of Steel". When they sent the record to me, I thought as well as everybody else thought, that the record was broke because he was the first one that came up with the scratching of records and running them backwards.

They didn't want to play that record because no one could really understand it. But we went to a club that's called Smitty's over in east St. Louis. Smitty would play anything for me 'cause he was the absolute boss, and I was his boy. I took it to Smitty's before I could get it to the radio, and man, they danced on that record.

So, by the time I saw what they were really doing to the record, I just went all out with "The Wheels of Steel". To this day, records are being spun backwards on record. I'm still amazed at how these guys could make records *talk*, switching them backwards and stopping them and then putting them back. They are still using that method that I believe Grandmaster Flash did himself—if he didn't create it, he was absolutely first with it. I see jocks today in clubs doing the same method in which Flash did on that record.

Speaking of Flash, he was a very unique person. As a matter of fact, he and I was very tight. Flash was so smart that he had charisma. Everybody would look for Flash to jump up on the stage and start, "rap, rap, rap, rap". Flash never did none of that in my presence, I recall. Maybe occasionally he may have said something. He could step on the stage, cross his arms, stomp his fist, do the little gestures that say, "I'm here, I'm king, I'm *Flash!*"

No doubt about it. You could get that impression of him and accept that, and it would be so thrilling to see him do the thing. It wasn't a case of arrogance, it was a case of being assured that, "I am one of the greatest of all times."

He gave that image to a lot of young rappers who took the method in which he conducted himself on the stage, live, and used it and embellished it to their benefit. That's why they began to have those types of poses – on stage and in the windows – that would make them send a message to their audience – now on TV, videos, live on the stage, and movies, wherever it is – that, "Hey, I'm here and I'm it. Ain't no better, won't be no better, was no better, and it will never be no better than what you see right here, right now. What you see is what you get, and what you're getting is the best that it is."

That's what Flash presented when he hit the stage, as far as my estimation was concerned. I loved it, and the women went *crazy*. Next thing I knew, Flash had gone his own separate way and Melle Mel had taken over. Now it was Melle Mel and The Furious Five. At first, it was Grandmaster Flash and The Furious Five. But, Flash, he ended up on television as a DJ for a major comedy show.

I remember I saw him once at a BRE convention. He was so glad to see me, man. I was so glad to see Flash, and it goes to show you that success don't change some people. Flash, as far as I'm concerned, was cool then with me. Last time I saw him, he was the same and he introduced me to everybody as "the guy that got him started," and I respect him and appreciate him for that.

I want to say, wherever he is at this point: "Grandmaster Flash, you are still my main man and one of the greatest record-spinning DJs I've ever known."

Back to my visit at Sugar Hill at this particular time. Joey took me to the studio, and he was beginning to record one of the artists from one of the hit groups called Sequence. Sequence was the first female rap group, as we all know, that had the record "Funk You Up" and many more. But there was a girl in that group that had a very unique and special talent. They all was excellent—could rap like you could never believe. No one could stand up against them because once they got to spitting that rap out, it was only proper. But they had a girl by the name of Angie B, a little girl from out of Columbia, South Carolina. As you know, there was three of them—Cheryl The Pearl, Blondie, and Angie B. Angie B was cutting a single record while I was there in the studio, and Joey said, "Hey, Gene, get in there with those boots, and say something on this record with Angie B."

Because they all loved me, I had such a relationship with all those youngsters that anything concerning me they was a hundred percent behind, because they knew that I had broke my heart, broke my back, broke myself, and my pocket to make sure that all of their records that I was affiliated with was gonna be a hit record. They knew if I had it, there was going to be some action with it.

So, Angie B was just so glad to get me on her first solo record. I think a said a couple or three words on it, and they put my name on the record, too, when it was released. The record turned out to be "Take Time to Make Time". That was her first single record, and she turned out to be a superstar on her own, as Angie Stone, who is now probably in the Hall of Fame. God bless her. She was my baby. I loved her.

As a matter of fact, I saw her overseas, and I pulled her up on the stage with me as I was singing along in the group Parliament Funkadelic (P-Funk) with George Clinton, and she rapped. Everybody was surprised she could still rap in being Angie Stone, and she got there and she rocked the house. We had such a wonderful time.

Back to the story, though. Sooner or later, the record finally came out. Joey sent me a copy of it and some money to go to Chicago and break the record, "Take Time to Make Time". So I got there; he sent me the records by airplane. I had to go out to the airport and pick the records up in a little package, like a mailing package, jumped in my little car that Joe had bought me, and drove to Chicago that night. That morning, I got to Chicago, I jumped on the damn ride, couldn't get off, then got lost trying to get over to the radio station. (I think it was WGCI.) And next thing I knew, I was almost in Wisconsin.

Before I knew it, I was in Milwaukee. I said, "Ohh, shit."

Joey was steady beeping me on my beeper, with the message, "What did they do? Did they like the record?" 'Cause he produced that record, I think—young Joey.

I got off. I went to a station called, "WAWA," W-A-W-A. I said, "Shit, since I'm in Milwaukee, I might as well work the record, since I'd have to double-back and go back to Chicago with the record."

'Cause I didn't have but the one acetate. It wasn't even the full version. It wasn't even a demo record. It was acetate, and they weighed about twenty pounds, it felt like, 'cause they had steel in the middle of them.

I took it to the radio station. I get a boy—I think the dude's name was Sir Walter (might have been his name) at the radio station. He was the program director. He knew me from Alvin Cash because I had played some clubs up there with Cash and The Crawlers. I think the play was called The Totem Pole or something like that. He was so excited to meet me because he had heard my reputation had gotten all over through the midwest and everywhere as being the dude that had been breaking them Sugar Hill records so fast by himself. He almost broke my arm to take that record and wanted to hear it. So I let him hear the record.

In the meantime, I called back to New Jersey and told Joey, "Man, I had made a mistake. I had took this record to Milwaukee instead of Chicago like you asked me to do."

I always wanted to do just what I was instructed to do because to be a good leader you gotta be a good follower. I know, the best way to keep a job, the best way to keep a good reputation, is to do what you commit yourself to doing. In other words, to do what you're told to do.

So Joey busted out laughing and said, "Man, you always do something that I'd never expect for you to do. Yeah, get the record played while your there. Break the record while you're in there, and then take the record back to Chicago. Have them go into the control room. Have the engineer make a cassette of it and he can play it and then you can take it along to Chicago."

The boy put the record on and got the credit for being the first radio station to play that Angie B record. I slid him a hundred dollars, jumped back in the car, headed back to Chicago, got up with the guys there, and took care of business. I went over to Pervis Spann and WVON that night, got the record played, went back to St. Louis, got the record played. Before you knew it, the girl had her first big hit record as Angie B—who did end up, as I said, Angie Stone.

A few weeks later, I get a word from Joey that her record was burning hot all over the country. I take a lot of pride in that record because my name is on it.

As time rolled by, I began to get more and more successful. My name started getting so big around my hometown St. Louis. You know, being in that situation I'm sure in most people's towns it's like that as far as they're concerned.

It's just like a bee in honey. Trouble will find you no matter how hard try to hide. Haters will come out and they will do their thing and let their presence be known. The haters begin to talk and try to set me up with a lot of things for a downfall because I was becoming so popular with the notoriety of being associated with all of these hit records, as well as being the number one entertainment columnist in the city of St. Louis which had stretched out, as I said, to a national recognition.

The paper had been increasing volume in subscriptions on the strength that people wanted to know who was going to be on the entertainment page this week and who was going to be the #1 record on the International Hook-Up record chart on there.

So, they start to sprinkle in salt to Skip at the distributor. "Skip, you know, Gene ought to do this and Gene ought to do that", so Skip was thinking that I was getting more out of it than I was getting, even though I was making a pretty good living out of it along with the records. Skip began asking me for a percentage on all of the people that he recommend that I could get on the chart for his benefit.

So we could never set horses with that because Skip didn't know nothin' about record charts and the newspaper. All he knew was about record sales or making deals with records and he was unbelievably, ultimately wise and successful with that. But, there was such a thing as inner greed, or a fact that this youngster done popped up out of nowhere and all of a sudden my name is bigger than he is. And he would create such a problem, that it was so uncomfortable to go to the record distributor to try to do some business directly with him and down there.

Lost in the Fast Lane

I decided to sever myself totally from the record distribution situation, period, and started working more out of my daddy's club, the International Hook-Up, and having them to send most of my records and all of my contacts and everything. And I was working out of the office upstairs over the club where my daddy had apartments up there for a lease by the week for different people that were coming to town. A few of my star friends would come and stay there, and he had some relatives that were staying up there.

So, I had a cousin that came from Mississippi. His name was Robert Earl. He hung around with me and saw how I was getting so much action with the newspapers and the promotion of these records. And he was a rap fan diehard, and he knew that Sugar Hill was undisputedly king, at least in my market. And so, he began to help me promote these records and start meeting people.

Somehow, he got hooked up with the gangsters in the town by being in the fast lane and not really knowing what was going on, but he thought he knew everything—a little country boy from Mississippi. And he started to getting girls with the records and he started going to different places and hanging with different people.

He got with some boys that I grew up with that had somehow turned real hard core gangster. Carrying guns, machine guns, and selling dope by the kilos and all kind of wild crazy shit that I had no affiliations with. But I was beginning to get associated with him, and that, because of him. And so, he had gotten to the point that he was starting to believe that he was a mobster in the middle of my notoriety as an entertainer and a record promoter with these rap records and this newspaper as an entertainment columnist.

First and foremost, everybody knew that he was my cousin—my stepmother's nephew. He was right there with us all of the time and people associated him directly with my family.

People was calling me and trying to meet me at my daddy's club every day for all kinds of things because my notoriety had over-exceeded what my expectations or anyone's expectations would have been from where I started with this thing. And it all happened because this rap record industry was blowing out of proportion and they couldn't stop it no more.

People would stop making the statement saying that this is going to be the last record, or ask is there going to be another one. They were saying, "Do you have another one? What's the new one?"

You know, it was more or less a case that everybody had created a whole new career, a whole revenue, a whole new social status and affiliations in this industry entertainment because of these rap records from coming up initially from Sugar Hill. And it would create an avenue for other elements to try to associate in your lifestyle.

And Robert Earl was sort of like an opportunity to use him to get to us and to get to me, primarily because of the notoriety of the newspapers and the TV. We got the television and all of the other kinds of media, that was, affiliations that had grown from the popularity of these Sugar Hill records that I was utilizing.

And, you know, this community was a very small community. These gangsters got ahold of Robert Earl because when he was out there with them they would say, "This is Gene Anderson's cousin, Robert Earl. You know, the guy with the rap records? The guy will the newspaper?" He would let that get to his head so, before you knew it, he'd begin to live like they was livin'. And, low and behold, the fast lane got him, grabbed him, and gobbled him up, and he began to shoot heroin.

I don't know how he ended up doin' that, but he began to shoot dope. And now, instead of a smile on his face, he's walkin' around with a frown on his face all the time. They was all tryin' to be the Godfather, with their big hats on and riding in the big cars and stuff, carrying pistols, and all kinds of madness.

I started to tell him, "Robert Earl, how did you manage to get yourself into all of this here? To this type of lifestyle?" He was hanging out with known gangsters – I know their names, but I won't say it – in our home town. One day I tried to pull him to the side and said, "Robert Earl, why don't you just get back with me, man, and deal with these records? I got new records comin' in and we can make a little money."

He didn't wanna hear none of that, because he was beyond promoting records and trying to be a star along with us, doing the entertainment thing. He was makin' more money with the heroin and the gangsters. And he had all the girls hangin' around, because they was all dope fiending now.

I said, "Man, you mean music can turn this kid from Mississippi into this... *wildlife?*" It was his first his first time with a lifestyle in the limelight, that this rap music had exposed him to it. Among other things, we were trying to get him on the right track again.

He, I had come to find out, was involved in the murder of a very popular young gangster. I think his name was Jeep. They had robbed Jeep for, I bet, a kilo of heroin and then killed Jeep and two or three other people.

He came back and he was so nervous and shaking. He was standing upstairs of my daddy's club and I said, "Robert Earl, what's goin' on witchu, man?" And my daddy was very upset because he knew what was going on, just not to the extent of it. But he knew Robert Earl was up to no good.

A friend of mine by the name of Arthur Qualls was a major faction in the underworld in St. Louis. We had grown up together, when we were kids. He would always call me Petey, from childhood.

"Petey—listen, man. Your cousin, Robert Earl, is out of hand. And everyone is talkin' about doing somethin' to him," he said, "I know you, man. You ain't into none of that—you a record man. You're pushing these records and everyone knows you from the newspapers and all that... Tell him to cool out, 'cause they got a contract on him."

I said, "A contract?!"

It was just *bizarre*. It was unbelievable.

But I couldn't stay out of the environment where Robert was at because he lived upstairs in the apartment over my daddy's club and, when I had left Skip, I started using the room upstairs as my office. All of my records from Sugar Hill, all of my newspaper stuff, and all my meetings was going on at my daddy's at International Hook-Up Lounge.

So there was no escape for *me*—we had to get rid of Robert Earl.

So I told Robert Earl, I said, "Listen man, you're gonna need to get on out of my daddy's apartment, and you're gonna have to move on from that type of lifestyle you're livin' 'cause you're in trouble, man."

He started with his mouth all turned down, he said, "Man, I ain't worried about none of this here. I can take care of myself."

He had guns all over the place. He had machine guns, sawed off shotgun on the mantelpiece, he got a pistol in a shoulder holster. This is *motion picture shit*. I can't believe that this young country boy – that was so nice and good looking, that everybody liked, that was a very good asset to me promoting records – had turned into a gangster.

He always had respect and love for me, and he was always respectful to my dad and everyone in our family. But outside of that he had became a straight *monster*, a real mad dog, and now killer associate.

So one night I was at the place and I was talking with an old blues singer that used to hang out with my daddy named Z. Z. Hill. He used to come and sit in the front window of my daddy's club and drink with my dad and talk–before he had this big, hit record, "Down Home Blues." I was telling him about Robert Earl, and he was telling me, he said, "Man, the best thing you can do is just keep doin' what you're doin' and just stay away from him."

I couldn't just stay away from him 'cause I love Robert Earl. I thought that he was just misguided, and the bright lights had got to him. He was believin' his own hype. I told him, "Robert Earl, please. Stay in for a while 'cause Arthur been by here and told me to why you up on what's goin' on."

Later on that night – after he had promised me that he was gonna stay out of the stream of this fast lane, stay upstairs in his apartment with his wife and his baby, and just cool down a while – he went out, and he came back up the steps with about four or five guys. We heard him on the steps by the side door of the nightclub. He went up there to the apartment–it was him, his brother-in-law, his wife, and two other guys. My brother, Jessie, went up there to see what was going on. They kind of played Jessie off to get him up out of there, so that's how I know who was up in the apartment at that time.

The next morning, about 10 o'clock in the morning, I get a phone call and they said, "Hurry down to the club. Somethin' bad happened."

I went down to the club, and Robert Earl had gotten murdered.

My son, who was about 8-years-old, had opened up the door and walked up there because he loved Robert Earl. Robert Earl would play with him all the time, and he went up to see Robert Earl Jr., who must have been not even a year old. He walked up there and he found everybody laying in a pool of blood, dead.

Robert Earl was in the kitchen and his brother-in-law was dead on the living room floor. Eula, who was his wife, was dead and laying on top of the baby in a pool of blood. The baby was drenched in blood when they found him under his mama. She apparently had gotten on top of Robert Jr. to stop them from shooting him, and the baby was so young that they just passed on him and didn't kill him.

Come to find out, the two guys that went upstairs with him – who was supposed to be his friends – took the contract, murdered Robert Earl, and got away.

I found out about it, went down to the club, and it was the most horrible scene I'd ever seen in my life. Blood was everywhere. Robert Earl had run to the kitchen, tryna' get out the back door, and they took the doorknob off and killed him right as he was tryna' jump off the back porch.

It really did break my heart to see him all bloodied up, shot up at the back door. I had begged him and said, "Please, Robert Earl. Change your ways."

By that time, the whole neighborhood was wondering what was goin' on up there, 'cause they knew that my office for Sugar Hill Records was in that building. They had been hanging out there, because International Hook-Up had been on TV and everything else. They knew that this was the headquarters for my promoting situation.

Now, this scar was all over my lifestyle and in my life. My cousin had got himself killed. And the gangsters that I did know, that I grew up with, was worried about me. They knew I had nothing to do with it, 'cause that wasn't my style of life, but they had been warning me about Robert Earl. That turned my whole world around.

Joe called me. He'd heard about it, and he called to ask me if I was okay and if I wanted to get out of there and move up to New Jersey with him. I didn't want to move to New Jersey. I could stay there, because I wasn't doing what was goin' on.

So Joe sent me an envelope full of hundred-dollar bills to take care of myself. It was to get started, to get up out of that area and open up my office someplace else. That's the kind of man that Joe Robinson was and the way he felt about me.

I took the money, yeah, but I never left. I just tried to stay there with my dad, keep things goin', and just turn the page.

From Promotion to Performance

After a little while, everything seemed to just die down. I was tryin' to get back to normal. But God has a way of straightening out problems that you can't figure out.

Somewhere along the line, some of those records that I'd been cuttin' and promoting by myself caught on. I went down to New Orleans because I had a friend by the name of Tommy T, and disc jockey E. Rodney Jones, who sent for me. I had a record that I had cut – that I was promoting at the same time I was promoting the Sugar Hill stuff – that had caught on *fire*.

So I thought I'd just give up promotion and go on tryin' to be a star, like I'd done prior to even foolin' with those records. The record caught on, and I had two at one time. One record was called "Joy" , by Gene Anderson, and after Scorpio had put out their record, "Scorpio" , everybody went electronic music crazy.

So I had an electronic record that I had cut, by the name of "Hey, Party People" by the Computer People Communicators. We called ourselves The CPC Group, and I had both of records at the same time. E. Rodney Jones was playing both songs at the same time, so I was out as two artists.

Mardi Gras time shows up, and Rodney gets us a gig down in the French Quarters. Tommy T is managing us. So we go down there and I get a band. I run into my old friend, Richard Dimple Fields, who helped me put the band together. We went and played the gig for Mardi Gras.

There were posters all over town. I got an outfit as "Zarbo

the Computer Man." There were lights all over it, and we had on gold lamé briefs, chest plates, tall crowns—real psychedelic-lookin' shit. The whole band has to dress up to the same likeness.

We had a lady by the name of Geneva Spikes to make all those outfits. It was futuristic stuff—looked like space stuff. I really got the idea from Flash Gordon and all that kind of stuff, then I had her make it.

So we did two gigs that night. I went as Gene Anderson. I wore a tuxedo—a nice, little, cute tuxedo that made me look like a pop star. I did the Joy record, "Baby, I Dig You," "Give Up the Poo Poo," and all my little stuff I had.

I'd done all that, then I went back in the dressing room for intermission, changed over, and put on this bizarre-lookin' outfit. The band changed clothes – the half of the band that was the rhythm section – and put on these space-lookin' outfits. We went out there and used the smoke screens and explosives, and we was playin' heavy metal and rock against electronic music. I had that pitch control voice, and it was just like the record. And the people went berserk.

After the show we was in the dressing room, and everybody comes into the dressing room wanting to get autographs and interviews. So, I'm down there as Gene Anderson, with my regular clothes on. They interviewed me and talked to me a little bit, but one young lady said, "Wait a minute..."

"We like you, Gene Anderson," she said, "But we wanna see this Zarbo, the computer man of the CPC."

I couldn't figure out what to do because I couldn't be two people at the same time.

"Well, that guy—you saw how bizarre and weird he was on stage," I said, "He don't like to interview. He sneaked out the back door and he's gone."

The little girl almost cried, she wanted to interview him

so bad. It was a big hoorah that he wasn't congenial enough to hang around and interview with all of the fans. Still somehow we had gotten away with the "scam" of being the same act, but *different*. Everything was goin' fine.

Selling Sugar Hill

Now, I'm doing good down there in Louisiana 'cause I've got a fresh start after all that drama with Robert Earl. Sugar Hill Records is rollin' good, I'm no longer with Skip and them, and my career looks like it's about to take off. My son was with my mom and he was okay, and I was tryin' to get back to my entertainer's lifestyle. Then one day, out of the clear blue sky, I get a phone call from Joe Robinson.

Joe calls me and says, "Gene, I got a big thing – a big thing – I want you to do for me." I heard some seriousness in his voice that I had never heard from Joe before.

"Man, this is huge," he said, "This is personal, just between me and you at this point in time. I don't want no one to know what it is. I'm gonna send you an airplane ticket, and I want you to fly up here and sit down and talk to me."

And you know when Joe says to come sit down and talk to him—you shut up, sit down, and talk to Joe. 'Cause Joe was a two-sided coin. On one side he's smilin' and, on the other side, he's serious. And he sounded so serious. I caught a plane and went to Joe.

Joe picks me up in a big Rolls Royce. He takes me to dinner, and we sit down and talk awhile. He says, "Listen, I'm gonna sell my company. I'm gonna sell it to Universal. I got Al Bell who's gonna make the deal for me."

I said, "Al Bell... Who's Al Bell?"

Al Bell was the president of Stacks Records and was, at one time, the president of Motown. He had made a deal for Motown with Universal. And I remembered that I had introduced Al Bell to Joe Robinson.

Joe Robinson had a big meeting with Dick Griffey, Sydney Miller, Huey Abner, and a bunch of other big-name guys at the Black Radio Exclusive (BRE) Magazine. And Al Bell was dyin' to meet Joe. He had never met Joe, and Joe was king. I had introduced Al to Joe, and Joe was reluctant to even talk to Al because Joe was rollin' so high and was doin' so much that he wasn't lookin' back. But I insisted and damn-near pleaded with Joe to meet and talk to Al.

Joe said that as soon as they finished the meeting, Joe was explaining how all of the heads of these small companies like Solar Records – not big like Warner Brothers, Polygram, and Capitol Records – had made a fool of themselves with the statement that they was braggin' on. They was braggin' on the fact that they had worldwide distribution from making one particular deal. Joe was explaining to them that each country is supposed to pay you individually for your product, instead of you just getting one blanket deal. When you've got one blanket deal, you've cheated yourself. But if you've got a deal with individual companies, you'd begin to get the true money like the big boys get it.

Their eyes opened up and they was overwhelmed that Joe was on top of them about that. He was showing them how to do business in a better way, because Joe was an absolute genius. Not only that, Joe was very informed on the "under" activities of the record business. He knew what the big boys knew, by being close to Morris Levi and all the rest of them. Joe had already been there, and Joe was not to be played with. Joe Robinson knew the game.

So, that's why he was kind of draggin' about going to see Al. But, in the midst of all that communication, I signaled to him and said, "Come on, please come and talk to Al."

He went there and talked to Al. Him and Al sat down, and after he really sat down and talked to Al, he found out that Al Bell was undisputedly a genius in marketing and recognizing the true record business. Al just didn't have a deal at that time because things that had closed up on his game in the record business. Joe exchanged numbers with Al and, from that moment on, him and Al became extremely close and talked to each other.

They talked about things because Joe could ask Al things that *he* didn't even know and Al had to answer. So, when it came down to a major deal of that sort, he went and got an expert in every capacity to consult him in a deal of this magnitude.

And the true reason that he sent for me is because he knew I could keep my mouth closed and do just what he said, and I could go to some of his independent distributors and collect the money that they owed him. They owed Joe almost a million dollars in money that they didn't pay him for the records that they had sold. And he knew that if they had found out that he was going to sell the company, he was not going to get a *dime* of his money!

So he sent me to represent him, to go and collect his money. I had less than a week, or less than ten days maybe, at the most to collect all of the money that I could from distributors across the country that he was affiliated with. Then I had to bring the money back to him before they found out that he was going to sell the company.

The deal was already made between him and the major record companies, but it hadn't been publicized yet and almost nobody knew about it but *me*!

So, I jumps on the airplane and the first thing I do is go down to New Orleans with Tommy T. This time, Tommy T had a big, gold Lincoln Continental limousine with black windows on it. You couldn't see in the limousine, not even hardly into the drivers window.

And so, I go in to Warren Hildebrand. Tommy T had told me, true or not, that Warren Hillabrand and them, those are the Dixie Mafia, and they don't care about nothing! They are hardcore gangsters. He told me to be careful what I say and how I act when I go in the place.

So, we sat there and we parked in front of the distributors and sit there about 10 or 15 minutes. People were going in and looking out the window 'cause you could see out on the front parking lot who was coming in. That was Mr. Hildebrand's office window, where he could see everything going in and out of his building of the distributorship. I know they was wondering, *Who's this big gold limousine, with these black windows, parked out in front of our place in this conspicuous spot for so long?*

I finally get out of the car... Boy I was so damn sharp. I was immaculate, because I knew I had to impress these people to get this money for Joe. So, I go in there and take Tommy T with me. Tommy T knew Warren Hillabrand, and those people in the distributor, because he had been doing records forever. He was runnin' things in New Orleans. So, he asked to speak to Warren and introduced me. He said, "This is Gene Anderson, Sugar Hill Records, and he would like to talk to Mr. Hillabrand. Joe Robinson sent him."

We sat down in the office for about 10 minutes or more. I began to get a little fidgety because I don't know if he knows what's going on. Joe just sent me in there knowing that I'm going to do whatever he tells me.

So, I finally get in there and Mr. Hillabrand meets me at the door. I sit down in front of the desk, and he sits back like he's Al Capone or somebody. He knows that if I'm affiliated with Joe Robinson it's a serious situation, because Joe don't come to see nobody or send nobody unless it's very serious.

And he's sizing me up! I'm a little guy. I'm young, but I'm sharp, and I'm looking serious. I talked to him real intelligently, and I also talked to him with authority, and I said, "Mr. Hillabrand, Joe sent me down here knowing that you are late on his payments on the records that he sold you, and he sent me down here to collect his money."

He said, "Well, Joe could have called me instead of sent you."

"Yeah, he wanted to make sure he got his money. That's why he sent me," I say, "Now listen, Joe says you owed him..." I forgot exactly, fifty or sixty thousand or whatever it was, and I said, "I got to go back with Joe's money. As far as you're concerned... I know your reputation..." I said, 'cause he was trying to be real brassy with me and was going to send me back with shit, with *nothing*!

But, he knows that if Joe sent somebody, they had to be qualified to get it!

"Listen, Mr. Hillabrand," I told him, "I ask you decently about giving me Joe's money. Now listen, it's almost noon I'm going to come back before three o'clock... You see that big limousine out there that you can't see in? I'm going to have three great big black dudes with me, with long black leather coats," – and it was about a hundred degrees out – "And when we come back through this door, you got to have our money. I appreciate who you are but I'm scared to death of Joe, and Joe said don't come back without it, Mr. Hillabrand. Have our money, thank you."

And I walked out the door with Tommy T. Tommy T was sweating like he was in a Turkish bath!

He said, "Man, why you talk to Warren Hillabrand like that for?"

I say, "Listen, man, what I told him was true. I ain't scared of Warren Hillabrand, but I know Joe don't play! Joe said don't come back without the money. Do you understand?"

We got to the limo, drove around a while. We went to the French Quarter for lunch and shit. My beeper goes off and it's Joe. I go to the phone booth and I call collect to Sugar

Hill. They finally get me to Joe, and Joe answers the phone and busts out laughing like a son of a bitch.

He said, "Man, I don't know what you said to Warren, but you shook his ass up. He asked me, 'Why did you send some crazy gangsta ass mother fucker down here to threaten me about that money? Joe, you knew I was gonna pay you.'"

Joe told him, "Yeah, well whatever he said he was gonna do, believe me—he was serious."

I got back there, and Warren Hillabrand gave me a briefcase – a *briefcase* – full of hundred dollar bills. And I had to sign a receipt. I signed it, got outta that place, went to the phone booth and called Joe.

I said, "I got the money, Joe."

"I knew you were gonna get it," he said. "Get on a plane, and go to Texas and see the Daily Brothers. They got so much money up there, so collect that money from them. Do it the same way you did Warren."

We called an airplane and went over to the Daily brothers.

And when I went to that grand, big, ol' Texas, they were some friendly people. But they was the mob, too. And I had told them the same spiel that Joe told me, but he'd already told them I was comin' to collect his money.

"And he got a brand new record," Joe told me to tell him, "And he's coming out with three new records." And I said he ain't gonna give it to 'em until they come up with some of the money that they owed him. They knew the reputation of Sugar Hill Records, so they gave me about 10 or 20 thousand and a cashier's check.

I got back on the phone, I jumped on the plane, and went to Shreveport, Louisiana—to talk to Stan Lewis. He had a place called Stan's Record Shops, I believe. Anyway, I had heard about him so much because he had radio stations that he was sponsoring. He had Wolfman Jack, and he also had

John Richbourg, who's name was John R.. They'd been playin' R&B Soul music all the way back in the Chess days.

So they had plenty of money, big money. They had big gangsta games goin' on with these records before I was born, probably. But anyway, I told him Joe sent me. Stan Lewis was so sweet and such a wonderful person, and he liked me so much because I had talked to him before on the phone about some other stuff. He just gave me the money for Joe right away. BANG BANG BANG! I think about 10, 15, 20 thousand.

I catch the plane and Joe says, "You got all the money?"

I said, "Yeah, Joe, I got a damn-near suitcase full of money."

He said, "Get on the plane and come on back."

I jumped on the plane. In those days they weren't x-rayin' you, your bags, and all that kinda shit. I got on the plane with *all that money.*

I think Joey picked me up at the airport and took me to the office. And when I went in the office, Joe was always surrounded by all them old record guys, hardcore gangsta guys like the Mad Hatter, Joe Medlin, as I've mentioned these guys before. Aubrey Taylor was there, and I don't know if Gus Redmond and them were there 'cause they was part of the gang.

But anyway, Joe put 'em out. I opened the suitcase and dumped the money up on the desk. Joe almost hollered, he was so proud of me. Joe reached in, gave me a handful of money—I'm his boy. I stayed around there a little while and then caught the plane, went back down to New Orleans.

The next thing I knew, it hit the news, it hit the train, in less than a week—"Joe Robinson Sold Sugar Hill Records to Universal."

The distributors went *berserk.* They was so upset that

they had gave that money to Joe and didn't know what was going on. They was hatin' on me like you wouldn't believe.

I laughed my ass off, because I knew that Joe was gonna cover me no matter what.

The Aftermath

After that, business became a little ho-hum for the Sugar Hill Gang. Joe moved out; Sylvia began to do her own thing. Joey Jr. seemed to be able to take over, and he was runnin' the company very effectively.

Joe got sick, somewhere along the line. Joe and his old friend, Ed Thompson, hooked up and they lived like two old senior citizens. Joe stayed into the record business, and dabbled a bit with the publishing, but basically the wild and exciting days of Sugar Hill seemed to just start fading away.

New companies started poppin' up, and so did different types of rap. Gangsta rap got huge. Other guys came in and made money, made their mark. You know, the White boys got in with Vanilla Ice. Before you knew it, rap became very mainstream.

People began to look at it as just like it's been there the whole time.

It seemed kind of amazing to me, because I remember how hard of a time that we had tryna get the records played or recognized—this art form of rap as a mainstream entity in entertainment.

I look back and I see all of these guys that made so many millions and millions of dollars in this business. They've got blue jeans, they've got all kinds of endorsements behind this Hip Hop.

I would have never dreamed that this would've happened, but I'm so thankful that it did happen. But there were some incidents here and there, concerning this rap business, that used to confuse me and piss me off about it.

For example, it got so big that one day I went to the Greek Theatre in Hollywood to see the Sugar Hill Gang and the whole rap entourage of original Sugar Hill guys. And we were sittin' in the back, in the dressing room area, and I was talkin' to Joey, Millie Mel, and Big Bank Hank. We was all sittin' around the table talkin' and some young White boy, some Harvard graduate, comes up and says, "Hey guy, what're you doin' back here?"

I looked at him and I said, "Whatchu mean, what am I doin' back here?"

"Well, nobody can be back here except the artists," he said, "You're gonna have to leave."

I said, "I ain't goin' no mother fuckin' where."

And, at that time, he looked at me as if he was gonna call security.

I asked Joey, "Who is this motha fucker?"

"He's the guy who's runnin' the rap tour," he said. "He's from the record company that's selling our records, the old catalog."

Joey jumped up and said, "What a minute, man. You can't talk to Gene Anderson like that! If it wasn't for Gene Anderson, none of us would have a job."

And I looked at the kid and said, "And you neither, you little motha fucker, you."

Everybody just busted out laughing. I was *pissed off*.

The dude looked at me and said, "Well *who* is he?"

And they said, "Well this was the guy that got us all started. You know, he's the one that broke these records–the ones we're out here makin' you rich from now. If it weren't for him, you wouldn't have no job to do this Hip Hop show."

So the guy looked at me, saw that I was so sharp, and he apologized and shook my hand. We talked for a little bit and he really found out who I was and what I had done. He went and got his partner and we all sat down and talked a little bit, sipped a little champagne. It kinda cooled off.

I left there that night thinkin' that it's so sad that all of the people that put the work in had nothing to do with this art form anymore.

Like Aubrey Taylor, and Joe Medlin, and Red Forbes. Like the Mad Hatter, and Gus Redmond and them, Deke Atkins, and Spiderman... A whole holster of guys that worked so hard and went through so much to make this company work and make this art form stand up.

These guys are all gone, most of 'em dead. I'm still here—been active, am still active, and gonna stay active in showbusiness. But it still breaks my heart to see that all of these guys, that did so much work to make Hip Hop come alive, are not around to see how big and huge it has gotten.

It is unbelievable. You've got people that is rappin' around the world. As a matter of fact, I recorded a girl in Moscow, Russia, by the name of Natasha Puvloff. She was the first female rap artist from Moscow to be successful. She had a record, that I produced, by her by the name of "Higher."

But I'm just sayin' that rap is goin' around the world. It's alive and should never die.

You know, I've got a lot of friends that have come into the rap business that are huge right now. They've got millions. And I remember when we all used to have to break off a piece of sandwich and ride on the bus, or cram into the station wagon to get to the next gig. Now, some of 'em have got private airplanes. That's so wonderful. God is good.

But I'd just like to say that whatever I was able to do to contribute to this wonderful art form, called *Hip Hop*, I was glad. I was hip enough to get with it, and I hopped on top of it, and I helped make it happen from day one.

"A hip, hop, a hippity-hop..." whatever you said, Wonder Mike!

Photo Gallery

So many of my fans, friends, and loved ones ask me to include these photos of some of the people, shows and situations that came to pass after my rise to worldwide fame due to me being part of the birth of Hip Hop. From the first day I began to help bring the "Rappers Delight" record alive, my life has never been the same. I think you will recognize some of these photos, like me as Gene Anderson and the International Hook-Up, with the Redd Foxx Show, The P-Funk All Stars, and ever my sparkling wine of the stars, a.k.a., the *ChamPooPoo*. And there are so many others—too many to name.

So I humbly ask you, my readers, to look and enjoy some of my life in photos. God is great everyday.

– Gene "Poo Poo Man" Anderson

Gene with mother; "Momma's Momma" Edna Boone

Gene and "Momma"

"Momma" – Jessi Anderson Gaither (in red)
with friend

A young Gene Anderson with Duke Ellington

Gene with "Daddy" – Jesse Anderson (sitting), and his childhood friend Mr. Ed, in St. Louis

Mr. & Mrs. Leonard Boone (left and sitting), LaVerne Boone (cousin), Gene Anderson, and his son Emanuel Howard

Granddaughters in St. Louis: Imani (l); Alena Howard (r)

Granddaughter Princesses

Gene with The Jackson Five, Randy OJ, Earl Pornail, at KATZ Radio

With Rick James, Rod 'Dr. Jockenstein' King, Big Ralph, others.

GENE ANDERSON AND THE INTERNATIONAL HOOK - UP

Management: International
Hook-Up Promotions
5082 Martin Luther King Drive
St. Louis, Mo.
314-361-9288

The International Hook-Up (l-to-r): Mary Anderson; Gene Anderson; Phyllis Williams

Gene with James Brown

Nancy Wilson and Gene Anderson

The Bar-Kays; Alvin Cash (in green); WESL crew with Dr. Jockenstein (front row in glasses), Andre 'Spider Man' Fuller (front row to his left); DJ Topcat (right of Gene)

(l-to-r) Gene, Randy OJ and friend, Ike Turner

Gene Anderson with Mohammed Ali and Al Waples

Gene with Antonio Fargas

Gene with Snoop Dogg

Stevie Wonder and Gene Anderson

Redd Foxx with Gene Anderson

Working with Redd Foxx for seven years

Ice Cube with Gene Anderson

(l-tor) Eddie Griffin, Floyd Mayweather Jr., Gene Anderson, Antonio Fargas

(l-r) Sly Stone, George Clinton, Gene Anderson

Gene with Amie Jo Greer and Flavor Flav

On stage with George Clinton, P-Funk

Gene and George Clinton

P-Funkin' with George Clinton

Gene with Keith Jackson at P-Funk Radio

In Hollywood (l-to-r): George Clinton; Gene Anderson; Eddie Griffin

Gene with Rick Warren, president and founder of the BMA

Gene playing "Sir Nose" at the Grammys with Parliament-Funkadelic with George Clinton (center) & Bootsy Collins (gold top hat)

GENE ANDERSON
INDUCTEE; INAUGURAL CLASS OF 2016

The Las Vegas

Black Music Hall Of Fame

Flamingo Library Theater
1401 E. Flamingo, Las Vegas
VIP Dining: 4:00 p.m. Showtime: 5:00 p.m.
Sunday October 9, 2016
To Attend Phone 702.583.9177

Gene with Joe Jackson

2018 BMA Hall of Fame

"Grandpa Gene" with his Hollywood God–Grandchildren

John Thomas, "greatest and favorite arranger, true genius"

Tribute Show, 2018 (portraying Buddy Holly, Cindy Lauper, Elvis, Rick James)

Filming of pilot for "Slick Willie's Used Cars"

The many looks of Poo Poo Man (Arnie G Designs Photography)

Gene Anderson's Sparkling Wine of the Stars – a.k.a. "ChamPooPoo"

First convention for champagne in Las Vegas: David Williams on Camera and Athana MacNeil (agent) behind Gene Anderson

Product display in China

Posing with the product (upper left clockwise): Flavor Flav; Samuel Jackson; Wolfgang Puck; Eddie Griffin and son; Quentin Tarantino

From commercial in Lee's Liquor Store in Las Vegas, featuring Joe Jackson

Gene recognized in 2013 by the USCGCC as a "civilian friendly ambassador between the US and China"

Gene with boxer Floyd Mayweather Jr.

In the studio with George Clinton, Bishop Don "Magic" Juan, Carlos "Sir Nose" McMurray, "Crazy" (girl) and others.

In Red Square, Moscow, wearing Czar Nicholas's cape & crown

Inspiration

This unknown slave is my inspiration and my hero, every day. With his look of personal pride, I know that if he survived, I will too. I would like to think his smile also shows pride in what I have accomplished in my own time.

Publisher's Note

The Birth of Hip Hop: "Rapper's Delight"–The Gene Anderson Story is the first of several books to be printed and available in *Amorphous Publishing Guild's* "Life & Times" series, devoted to telling history through personal biography and giving witness to both. These narratives are as honest as any, told from the memories and perspectives of authors in the way only someone there could tell it.

This particular book was written entirely through voice transcription, and every effort was made to be true to the unique voice and intention of the author with only the most necessary edits. There will be no apology for what some may consider improper grammar, as the language preserved here is a legitimate and longstanding American dialect, as important to the times and culture of the subject matter as any other detail.

Over these forty years, Hip Hop has defined African-American achievement in the American music industry, with an appeal that has transcended and even built bridges in terms of race, age, and national boundaries. But history is ultimately about *people*. There are so many individuals who have been instrumental in the times and places we know about, and their stories go untold. When told, those of us who are too young or not immersed in the culture can see it fresh, through eyes that were both behind the scenes and aware of social circumstances that may never be taught in a classroom.

When my daughter, Christina Stock, the book's transcriptionist and primary editor, was introduced to Gene, she was not as familiar with the genre and its early days. Yet, she loved getting to know Gene through his story—and learn about the roots of Hip Hop along the way. Her generation inherited it as a fully established, internationally recognized genre. On the other hand, my generation grew up listening to the music and artists mentioned in this book. Personally, I wore out cassette tapes and dared to boogaloo at high school dances. I also recently discovered that my wife had owned a vinyl copy of "Rapper's delight" (the blue label).

Through her transcription work, she shared these stories with me, adding a personal dimension to what I knew as Rap and Breakdancing music "back in the day." A generation apart, we agree that Gene's story needs to be told and preserved for every generation of musicians and fans.

That is one of many reasons why it has been such a pleasure to work with Gene "Poo Poo Man" Anderson. For that, and trusting us to do our best in making this book a reality, the author has our utmost personal gratitude.

We hope you, the reader, get as much enjoyment from this book as we had making it available to you.

Ken JP Stuczynski
Amorphous Publishing Guild, Publisher
Christina E. Stock
Transcriptionist and Editor

CPSIA information can be obtained
at www.ICGtesting.com
Printed in the USA
BVHW050026100120
569039BV00003B/18/P